TEACHING & DISCUSSION

St. Orsisius of Tabenna

Translated by: D.P. Curtin

Dalcassian Publishing Company

TEACHING & DISCUSSION

Copyright @ 2008 Dalcassian Publishing Company

All rights reserved. No part of this publication may be reproduced, distributed, or transmitted in any form or by any means, including photocopying, recording, or other electronic or mechanical methods, without the prior written permission of the publisher, except in the case of brief quotations embodied in critical reviews and certain other non-commercial uses permitted by copyright law. For permission request, write to Dalcassian Publishing Company at dalcassianpublishing at gmail.com

ISBN: 979-8-8690-9252-6 (Paperback)

Library of Congress Control Number:
Author: Curtin, D.P. (1985-)

Printed by Ingram Content Group, 1 Ingram Blvd, La Vergne, Tennessee

First printing edition 2008.

TEACHING & DISCUSSION

TEACHING & DISCUSSION

TEACHING & DISCUSSION

I. Hear, O Israel, the commandments of life; perceive with the ears, and understand prudence. What is it, Israel, that you are in the land of enemies? You have grown old in a foreign land; you are stained with the dead; you have been compared with those who are in hell, and you have forsaken the source of wisdom. If you had walked in the way of God, perhaps you would have lived in peace. Learn therefore, says he, where is thy prudence, where is the strength of glory and virtue, where is intelligence, where is the law of the eyes, and peace. Who found its place, and who entered its treasures (Bar. 3)? Baruch spoke these things on behalf of those who were taken into captivity in the land of Babylon and their enemies, because they did not want to receive the commands of the prophets, and they forgot the law of God, which was given through Moses. For this reason, God brought upon them punishments and executions, and brought them under the yoke of captivity: therefore training them as his own, and like a father correcting his children, not wanting the corrected to perish, but desiring to save them through repentance.

II. Whence we also ought to remember the words of the Apostles, who said: If nature spares not the branches, nor spares us (Rom. 11), and we neglect to fulfill God's precepts? All these things happened to them in figures: but they were written for our correction, in which they came to the ends of the ages (1 Cor. 10). And indeed, they were transferred from the city of Judah to the city of the Chaldeans, changing their places in the country; and abandoning joy, let us give into the captivity of punishments, and lose the eternal joy which our fathers and brothers found with unsteady labor.

III. Therefore let us not be overcome by forgetfulness and let us not consider ignorance the patience of God, who therefore sustains and defers, so that when we are converted to better things, we are not delivered up to torments. When we sin, we do not think that God agrees with our sins, because He does not immediately take revenge; but let us think of the fact that, soon going out of the world, we shall be separated in the future from our fathers and brothers, who possess the place of victory. Whom we shall have, if we choose to tread in their footsteps, and pay attention to the fact that the Apostle Paul here also separates the saints from the sinners and delivers the transgressors to the destruction of the flesh, that the spirit may be saved (1 Cor. 5). Blessed is the man who fears the Lord, and whom he reproves to be reformed, and teaches him his law, that he may walk in his commandments all the days of his life, who does not grumble for his sin.

IV. Therefore let us also examine our ways, and judge our proper steps; and let us return to the Lord, and lift up our hearts with our hands to the highest and to heaven: that in the day of judgment he may be our helper, and that we may not be confounded when we speak to our enemies at the gate, but that we may be more worthy to hear it: Open the gates, that the people who guard may enter justice and truth (Judg. 15). He who has the truth of the heart, and he who possesses peace, can say: Because we have hoped in you, Lord, forever. Let us remember the Lord, and let Jerusalem rise above our hearts. Let us not forget that man of whom it is written: Blessed is the man who trusts in the Lord, whose hope is in him. It will be like a fruitful tree by the waters, and it sends out its roots to the moisture: it will not be afraid when the heat comes, and will have leafy branches, and in the time of drought it will grow, sprouting fruit. There is a heavy heart in all, and there is a man, and who knows him? Therefore, the Lord is searching for hearts and minds, that I may repay each one according to his ways (Jer. 17).

V. Let us remember our own, and not despise the offenses which we have committed; and let us go through each commandment of our Father and of those who have taught us, with an anxious heart: not only believing in Christ, but also patient for him, and knowing that of which it is said: The Spirit of our countenance is Christ the Lord (Thren. 4). And elsewhere: Thy law is a lamp unto my feet, and a light unto my paths. And again: The word of the Lord quickened me, and the law of the Lord undefiled, converting souls. The clear commandment of the Lord, enlightening the eyes (Psalm 118). And the apostle says, the law is holy, and the commandment is holy, and just, and good (Rom. 7). Understanding all this, we will be worthy to hear: When the righteous man falls, he will not be hurt, because the Lord upholds his hand (Psalm 36). And again: The just shall fall seven times and rise again (1 Peter 3).

VI. Now, then, brothers, working patiently with God and challenging us to repentance, let us wake up from a deep sleep, because our adversary is like a roaring lion, seeking whom he may devour (1 Pet. 5). . Let us not fail in laboring and sowing the seeds of virtue, so that in the future we may reap joys, and let us listen to the teaching of Paul: But you who have kept the teaching, learning, study, patience, persecution, and following the examples of the saints, let us continue in what we have begun, having Jesus as our prince and perfecter. Let us understand the hair of our head on the way, that it may be perfume in our beard, that it may reach the hem of our garment, that we may fulfill all that is written (Psalm 132).

VII. Wherefore, O leaders and superiors of monasteries and houses, in which men have been trusted, and among whom T, or E, or A, as I may say in common, in whom men have been trusted, let each one with his troops wait for the coming of the Savior, that at his sight they may be adorned with arms prepare an army Do not cool them in carnal things, and do not give them spiritual food. Or teach them spiritual things again, and be afflicted in carnal things, that is, in food and clothing. But give both spiritual and carnal food alike and give them no occasion for negligence. Or what is this justice, that we afflict our brethren with labor, and ourselves have leisure? or else we may impose on them a yoke which we cannot bear ourselves. We read in the Gospel: according to the measure of your month it will be repaid to you (Matt. 7). Wherefore let us have labor and refreshments in common with them and let us not think of the disciples as slaves, and let their tribulation be our joy; Lest the evangelist rebuke us with the Pharisees: Woe unto you scribes, who bind burdens to be borne, and lay them upon men's shoulders, and yourselves dare not even touch them with a finger (Matt. 23).

VIII. There are some who pay attention to themselves, as living according to God's command, they speak to themselves and say: What have I to do with others? As for me, that I may serve God and fulfill his commandments, it does not concern me what others do. Ezekiel rebuked this, saying: O shepherds of Israel, do the shepherds feed themselves? don't they feed the sheep? Behold, you have eaten milk, and covered yourself with wool, you have not sacrificed what is fat, and what is weak you have not strengthened; what is broken you do not bind; You did not bring back what was wrong; You did not ask that it had perished; as it was, you caused me to fail in labor, and scattered my sheep, because they had no shepherds (Ezek. 34). Therefore, the Lord himself will come with his elders and princes, and that will be fulfilled in us: Your pursuers will spoil you, and those who return will make you go astray (Is. 3). Rather, we should hear more: Blessed is the land, whose king is the son: your nobles and princes in time will eat in strength and will not be put to shame (Eccl. 10).

IX. Therefore, O man, do not cease to admonish even one soul that is entrusted to you, and to teach what is holy, and to set yourself an example of good works, and be careful as much as possible that you do not love one and hate another, but also show equality to all: lest perhaps God hates whom you love, and God

TEACHING & DISCUSSION

loves whom you hate. Agree with no one who wanders for friendship, and oppress one, and relieve another, and let your labor perish. Sitting in the humbler places, in which our Father commands us not to sit at all, let the superiors of the houses take care, lest perhaps any one of the brethren do an injury to the superior, and he, being angry, discerns and says: What cause have I to the contemptible man? Let him do what he wills, it does not concern me; I neither admonish him, nor correct the erring, whether he be saved or perished, it does not concern me. O man, what are you talking about? Understand with what fury you are overcome, and hatred has seized your heart, so that your brother perishes more by your fault than by his sin; to whom you must forgive, and receive him who is penitent, so that you may say that of the Gospel: Forgive us our debts, as we also forgive our debtors (Matt. 6). If, then, you want God to forgive you your sins, and you to forgive your brother whatever it is that he has sinned against you, remember that commandment: Do not hate your brother in your heart (Luke 11). And Solomon's admonition: Raise up your citizen for whom you have promised (Prov. 6). And again: Do not cease to train a child, for if you strike him with a rod, he will not die (Prov. 23). Listen also to Moses saying: You shall rebuke your neighbor with rebuke, lest you incur sin on his behalf (Leviticus 19). Let not that of Solomon happen again: He who does not warn his son to keep himself from perdition, will be quickly dissolved (Prov. 19).

X. All those to whom the care of the brethren is entrusted, brace themselves for the coming of the Savior and his fearful judgment seat. For if to give account for oneself is full of discrimination and fear, how much more to undergo torture for the fault of another, and to fall into the hands of the living God? Nor can we obtain ignorance, when it is written: God will bring every deed into judgment, in all that is neglected, whether good or bad (Eccl. 12). And we read in the Apostle: We must all appear before the judgment seat of Christ, so that each one may receive for what he has done, whether good or bad (2 Cor. 5). Isaiah also signifies the appointed day in which God will judge the world of the earth in justice, saying: Behold, the day of the Lord is coming, incurable of fury and wrath, to set the world of the earth in a wilderness, and to destroy the sinners from it (Isaiah 3). We know that all that is written in the law, and the prophecies of the prophets have foretold us; our holy Father also taught us, that we are to keep and give an account of each, why we did not do them, or we did them more negligently. For it is spoken to whom all judgment has been delivered from the Father, and the truth teaches the truth: You do not believe that I accuse you to the Father; Moses is the one who accused you, in whom you hope. For if you believed Moses, you would also believe me: for he wrote about me (John 4).

XI. From all of which we learn that it is necessary for us to stand before the judgment seat of Christ, and to be judged of each individual, not only by our works, but also by our thoughts; And this is not only to be heard from the superiors of houses, but also from the princes of monasteries, and from each brother who is counted among the common people: for all must bear one another's burdens, that they may fulfill the law of Christ (Gal. 6), and hear the Apostle writing to Timothy: O Timothy, guard the deposit, avoiding profane new words and the profession of a false name of knowledge (1 Tim. 6). And we have a deposit handed down from God, in the conduct of the brethren, for whom we labor and await future rewards: lest perhaps it should be said to us also: Let this people go, that they may depart (Exod. 5); and those who forsake the traditions of our Father are charged: Those who have the law do not know me, the shepherds have acted wickedly against me (Jer. 2). Wherefore he reproved others, saying: I have placed my inheritance in your hand, but you have not shown any mercy: you have burdened the old with a yoke (Isaiah 47). And it is necessary for us not only to hear, but also to understand: for he that is ignorant shall be ignorant. And in another place, it is written: Because thou hast rejected my knowledge, and I will reject thee, that thou shouldst not serve as a priest to me (Hosea 4).

XII. Therefore, dearest brothers, who follow the life and precepts of the convents, stand in the rapture once intended, and fulfill the work of God, so that the Father, who first instituted the convents, may joyfully speak for us to the Lord: As I was handed over to them, so they live. The apostle also spoke the same while he was still in the body: I praise you because you remember me in everything, and you have kept my traditions as I delivered them to you (1 Cor. 11).

XIII. And you, then, the leaders of the monasteries, be anxious, and use all care for the brethren with the fear and justice of God: do not abuse your power in executions but set an example for all and the subordinate flock. just as our Lord set himself an example in all things, who set up families like sheep: that you may have mercy on your flock by faith and remember the apostolic sentence in which he says: I have withheld nothing, so as not to declare to you all the will of God. And again: I did not stop beseeching each one of you, and teaching you publicly (Acts 20). See how much heart and how much mercy there was in the man of God, who was not only concerned for all the churches, but languished with the languishing, and bore the sufferings of all. Let us be careful, lest through our negligence someone should stumble and fall, and let us forget the words of the Lord our Savior, who speaks in the Gospel: Father, whom you have given me, I have not lost any of them (John 17). Let us not despise any soul, lest everyone perish by our hardness. For if someone dies because of us, our soul will be held responsible for his soul. Indeed, our Father used to incessantly emphasize this to us, and warned us not to fulfill that saying in us: Each one oppresses his neighbor: and again: If you bite and devour one another, see that you do not consume one another (Gal. 5). From which it appears that he who preserves the soul of another is the guardian of his own soul.

XIV. But you who are of the second order of the monastery, show yourselves first in virtue, lest anyone perish by your vice. Don't fall into that reproach into which he falls who eats and drinks with drunkards and does not give food to his fellows in his season, where there is weeping and gnashing of teeth (Matt. 24). Lest such a condemnation should seize those of you, but when the times of refreshment come we deserve to hear: Hail, good and faithful servant: because you have been faithful over a little, I will set you over much, enter into the joy of your Lord (Luke 19).

XV. You also, the leaders of individual houses, be ready to answer all those who demand from you an account of the faith that is in you. Warn those who are disorderly; comfort the little souls; support the weak; Be patient with all, and listen to the Apostle's admonition: And you, fathers, do not provoke your children to anger, but nurture them in the discipline and admonition of the Lord (Eph. 6), and know that to whom more is given, more will be required of him; and to whom more is believed, more will be required (Luke 12). And consider not only those things which benefit you, but those which benefit your neighbors, and let the Scripture be fulfilled in you, saying: Because you follow the benefit of your own house, therefore the heaven will withhold its dew, and the earth will not give its fruits, because you have weighed down your words against me (King 1). It is also said elsewhere: Because you did not do it to one of the least of these, neither did you do it to me (Matt. 25).

XVI. I will often say, and repeat the same thing: Be careful not to love others and hate others; do not support this and neglect that; and let thy labor be found undone, and all sweat perish; and when you have come out of the body and freed from the whirlwind of this world, you will think that you will enter the harbor at rest; then you will find the wreckage of injustice, and in what measure you have been measured, may it be remitted to you by him who does not accept persons in judgment. If anything mortal, or something shameful, has been committed in the houses through the negligence of the Superiors, after their own executions, the Superior will also be held guilty of the crime: which our Father of holy memory was always wont to instill in us.

XVII. Wherefore with all care and concern let each keep the flock entrusted to him, and imitate the shepherds of the Gospel, to whom the Angel of God came not sleeping, but watching, and announced to them the coming of the Savior (Luke 2). He himself says: A good shepherd lays down his life for his sheep: but he that is hired is not a shepherd, whose sheep are not; and it does not concern him about the sheep (John 12). Luke's history writes about the good shepherds: Now there were shepherds who observed and kept watch over their flock by night. and the angel of the Lord came to them, and the glory of God shone around them, and they were afraid with great fear; And the angel said to them: Fear not: for behold, I bring you good tidings of great joy, which shall be to all the people: for a Savior has been born to you today, who is Christ the Lord in the city of David. And this will be a sign for you, you will find a baby wrapped in swaddling clothes and laid in a manger (Luke 2). Were they alone at that time feeding the sheep, and following the flock through the wilderness? But since they alone were anxious, and the fear of wolves lying in wait overcame the natural night's sleep, they deserved to be the first to hear that it was near: but Jerusalem was asleep and ignorant. Hence David also says: Behold, he who guards Israel will not sleep (Ps. 70). Therefore, you also watch with trembling and fear, working out your salvation, and knowing that the Lord of the universe, through whom all flesh receives whatever has been worked, appeared to the apostles alone after the resurrection, and said to the chief of the apostles, Peter: Simon of John, do you love me more than these? He answered him: Lord, you know that I love you. Jesus said to him: Feed my lambs. He says to him again the second time: Simon of John, do you love me? He answered him: Yes, Lord, you know that I love you. He says to him: Feed my sheep (John 21). Thirdly, he commanded to feed the sheep: and in that he enjoined us all this duty, that we should carefully feed the Lord's sheep, and on the day of his visitation we should receive for labor and care, which he promised us in the Gospel, saying? Father, I will that I be there, and they be with me. And again: Where I am, where my servant will be also (John 12). Let us look to the promises and to the rewards of the faithful, let us bear all labor more easily, walking as the Lord himself walked, who is the promiser of rewards.

XVIII. You also who are second to individual houses, follow humility and modesty, and consider the individual precepts of the elders as the norm of common life, so that in preserving them you may preserve your souls, and be like him who says: My soul is always in my hands (Ps. 118). The Son will glorify the Father and rejoice in your fruits: for without works and fruits no one will be happy in the company of the Lord: so that when you have fruit in the Lord, you may inherit and co-inherit with Him.

XIX. But all you brethren, who are subject to the order of free servitude, have your loins girded, and burning lamps in your hands, like servants who wait for their master when he returns from the wedding, so that when he comes and knocks, they may immediately open to him. Blessed are the servants whom the coming Lord finds watching (Luke 11). So shall it be unto you, if the long labor do not work weariness in you, you shall be called to the heavenly banquet, and the angels shall minister to you. These are the promises of those who keep the commandments of God, and these are the rewards of the future. Rejoice in the Lord; I say again, rejoice (Phil. 4). Subjected to the Fathers with all obedience; without murmurings and various thoughts, carrying the simplicity of the soul to good works, so that, full of virtue and fear of God, you may be made worthy of God's adoption. Take the shield of faith, in which you can withstand all the

TEACHING & DISCUSSION

fiery arrows of the devil, and the sword of the Spirit, which is the word of God (Eph. 6). Be wise as serpents, and simple as doves (Matthew 10). Listen to Paul speaking: Children, obey your parents (Col. 3), and obtain the salvation of your souls through those who are in charge of you. And in another place, it is also written: Submit to your leaders and submit, because they are watching over your souls, giving an account for you (1 Cor. 3). And always fear what the same apostle says: You are the temple of God, and the Spirit of the Lord dwells in you. But if anyone violates the temple of God, God will destroy him (Eph. 4). And again: Do not grieve the Holy Spirit of God, in whom you are sealed for the day of redemption of the righteous judgment (Ibid.).

XX. Keep the chastity of your body, as if you were a closed garden, a sealed spring (Cant. 6). For he who is born of God does not sin, because his seed remains in him (1 John 3). John says the same thing: I am writing to you, young men, because you are strong, and the word of God abides in you, and you have overcome the evil one (1 John 2). When you too have conquered the enemy, God giving you help, then he too will say: I will rescue them from hell and redeem them from death. Where is your contention, death? Where is your stimulus, death (Hosea, 13)? But if we devour death, we shall overcome it, and it will be said to us: Death shall by no means have dominion over it (Rom. 6): because the death by which we once died in sin is dead in us, and the life which we live in Christ we live forever (Rom. 7). For he who dies in the flesh will be justified from sin. Let us no longer live in the desires of men but let us fulfill the rest of our lives in the will of God. Those who fear the Lord arm yourselves with chastity, that you may deserve to hear: But you are not in the flesh, but in the spirit (Ibid.). And know that the perfect are given to the perfect, and the empty are returned to the empty, according to the Gospel saying: To him who has, more will be given, and he will have an abundance; but he that hath not, and that which seemed to have, shall be taken from him (Mark iv.). Let us imitate the wise virgins who deserved to enter the chamber with the bridegroom, who had in their vessels and lamps the oil of good works. Furthermore, the foolish virgins found the chamber door closed, because they refused to prepare oil for themselves before the wedding (Matt. 25). These things happened to them in shape; for they were written for our correction (1 Cor. 10), so that we may avoid the old ones and keep the precepts of the wise man, who said: My son, if your heart is wise, you will make my heart rejoice,

TEACHING & DISCUSSION

and my lips will remember your words (Prov. 23). if, however, they were right. And again: Let not your heart be envious of sinners but be in the fear of God all day long and observe the worship of God constantly (Prov. 23).

XXI. Let us watch more attentively and let us know that God has given us great grace through our Father Pachomius, that we may renounce the world; and we would put all the cares of the world and the cares of worldly things as nothing. What opportunity has been left to us, that we may have anything of our own, from a cord to mending our shoes; when shall we have superiors, who are anxious for us with fear and trembling, both in food, and in clothing, and in sickness of the body, if by chance it should occur, that we may fear nothing, and by occasion lose the profits of the flesh and soul? We are free, we have thrown from our necks the yoke of worldly servitude; why do we want to return to our vomit again, and have something to worry about and fear to lose? What is the use of a superfluous shawl, or cleaner meals, or a better bed? when all things are prepared in common, and nothing is harder than the cross of Christ, according to which our living fathers built us on the foundation of the apostles and prophets, and the discipline of the gospels, which is contained in the corner stone of the Lord Jesus Christ (Eph. 2): We descend to a life of humility, exchanging riches for poverty, and delights for simple food.

XXII. Do not, I beseech you, forget the purpose once taken, and let us consider the traditions of our Father as ladders leading to the kingdoms of heaven. Do not long for what you have trod before. It is sufficient for us to have, as is sufficient for a man, two coats of mail, and another worn, and a cloak of line, two hoods, a belt of line, breeches, a skin, and a staff. To whom some service and dispensation is entrusted to the monastery, and if he makes a profit from it, it will be thought a crime and a sacrilege to touch anything from it and turn it into his own rest, as if looking down on those who have none and are rich in happy poverty: so that not only he himself perishes, but and will challenge the others to achieve it. And indeed, those who bowed their necks, and with all humility and affliction mourned and lamented in the presence of God, when they have come out of this body, they will be led and lie down with the holy fathers Abraham, Isaac, and Jacob, prophets, and apostles, and worthy of consolation they will enjoy themselves, just as Lazarus enjoyed himself in Abraham's bosom. But those who lived in a convent and diverted something from the common to their own use, woe to them when it leaves the body, it will be said to them: Remember, because you received good things in your life (Luke 16); to the laboring brethren, and fasting and abstinence, and sweating with incessant labor. Wherefore see them in joy and gladness, who have left the present life, that they may attain the future: but you are set in squalor and torments, and misery, because you would not hear the gospel discourse, and despised the words of Isaiah, saying: Behold, they that serve me shall eat, but you shall be hungry. Behold, those who serve me will drink, but you will be thirsty. Behold, those who serve me will rejoice, and you will cry because of the pain of your heart and howl because of the broken spirit (Isaiah 65). You have heard all the beatitudes of the Scriptures, and you would not receive instruction.

XXIII. Therefore, brothers, let us be equal, from the least to the greatest, both rich and poor, in perfect harmony and humility, so that it may be said of you also: He who had much, did not abound; He who has little does not need (2 Cor. 8). Let no one provide for his own pleasures, seeing his brother in poverty and distress, and say to him the prophetic saying: Did not God create you one? Is not the Father one of you all? Why hast thou forsaken every man his brother, that they might make abominable the testament of your fathers? Judah was abandoned, but Israel became an abomination (Malachi 2). Therefore, according to what the Lord and Savior commanded the apostles, saying: I give you a new commandment, that you love one another as I have loved you: and by this you will know that you are truly my disciples (John 13); we must love one another, and show that we are truly servants of the Lord Jesus Christ, and sons of Pachomia, and disciples of the coenobies.

XXIV. If the head of the house rebukes someone from among the brothers who are subject to him, training him in the fear of God and desiring to correct him from error, and another wants to speak for him and defend him, subverting his heart; he who does this sins to his own soul, because he overthrew him who could be corrected, and casts the rebel down to the ground, and by evil persuasion has deceived him who was tending to better things, leading himself astray and causing others to err. To this it will be adapted accordingly: "Woe to him who gives drink to his neighbor, a tumultuous subversion, and intoxicating him" (Habakkuk 2). Woe to him who causes the blind to err in the way (Deut. 27). Whoever offends any of those who believe in God, it is expedient for him that a donkey's millstone be hung around his neck and he be thrown into the sea (Matthew 18). Because, as we have said, he overthrew the one who lifted himself up, and transferred the obedient to pride, and he turned him who could walk in the sweetness of charity into bitterness; and he corrupted the subject by the laws of the monastery, by evil counsels, and caused him to hate him, and to be grieved against him, who taught him the discipline of the Lord, bringing disputes and discords between the brethren, and not fearing that which is written: Who art thou that judgeth another man's law? He stands or falls to his master. But he will stand, and the Lord is able to set him up again (Rom. 14). Consider what he said: But the Lord is able to establish him. He is not powerful who ignores the words of the Lord.

XXV. Wherefore, brethren, let us greatly avoid subverting the mind of any one against his teacher and tutor; and let us remember the Scriptures that say: Free your heart from malice, that you may be saved (Jer. 4). And instead of obedience, let us not sow pride and stubbornness in our hearts. For he who fears his Lord, if he sees his brother go astray and slip, should rather point out what is holy and point out the right way, so that, walking with all the chastity and trembling of God, he may carry out that sentence of Solomon: Deliver those who are led to death and redeem from Thou shalt not cease from slaughter (Prov. 23) Nor say, I do not know this man. Know that God knows the hearts of all. And Jude speaks in his Epistle: And these indeed they snatched from the fire, and having a coat stained with hate (Jude 1). Let us beware of this kind of clothing and let us rather put on the armor of God, that we may be able to resist against the wiles of the devil. For our battle is not against flesh and blood, but against powers and principalities, against the rulers of this darkness, against spiritual wickedness in the heavenly places (Eph. 6).

XXVI. This, too, must be especially taken care of, that no one should recommend anything to another's house or cell, and should cause discipline against the monastery. He who is like this is not among the brethren, but a hireling and a sojourner; nor should he eat at the Lord's Passover among the saints, because he became a stumbling block in the monastery, and of him it might be said: Cast the stones out of my way (Jer. 20). For if our clothes, when we wash them, are not dry, we have no power to keep them with us until the evening, and we give the steward to whom we are entrusted, or to him to whom the storeroom is entrusted, to carry them to that place where the clothes of all are reserved alike, and in the morning to us they are given, that we may spread them out in the sun, and when they are dry, we do not keep them with us, but give them to be kept in common, according to the precepts of the elders; how much more, if you entrust to another those things which you are properly seen to possess, or wish to be in your own power, you sin against the discipline of the monastery, and do not understand Paul speaking to you: But you were called to liberty, so much so that you do not abuse your liberty for the occasion of the flesh, but serve in charity one another (Gal. 5). And again: The Lord is near, do not be anxious, but be attentive in prayer and supplications (Phil. 4). Let him also know that he who has received a commendation from another, and thinks he is doing the pious thing, in order to cool his brother, that he is sinning against his own soul, by subverting the rule of the monastery. O fool, your soul is entrusted to your guardian, and he who guards your soul and body will be considered unworthy to preserve it from destruction? Let us love righteousness, that we may be justified. For we read: Mercy meets those who practice truth.

XXVII. This also must be observed, lest anyone deceived by a foolish thought, nay, entangled by the devil's snares, should say in his heart: When I die, then I will give to my brothers what I have. O most foolish man, where did you find this written? Did not all the saints serving God at once lay down all the baggage of the world? Was it not in the Acts of the Apostles that they brought all that they had to the feet of the Apostles (Acts 4)? Or how can you put on the garment of righteousness when you are dead, who did not deserve to have it alive? Why have you forgotten that which is written: What a man sows, that shall he also reap (Gal. 6); and, each one shall receive according to what he has done (Ephes. 6); and, He will repay each one according to his works (Rom. 2); and again: I, the Lord, searching the hearts and testing the reins, that I may render to each one according to his ways, and according to the fruit of his inventions (Psal. 61)? Why are you not yet engaged in life, and being established in this little body, do you not hear David speaking: He lays up treasures, and does not know to whom he gathers them (Ps. 145), and the gospel discourse, rebuking the avaricious: Fool, this night they seek your soul:

TEACHING & DISCUSSION

but what you have prepared, whose will they be (Luke 12)? And again: In that day all their thoughts shall perish. Fool, why don't you want to hear the Lord exhorting: Go, sell all that you have and give to the poor, and take up your cross and come, follow me (Matthew 19)? When the youth heard this, he turned back; for his heart was not right, and therefore he could not lay down his heavy burden of riches. He indeed had the will, and the Scripture testifies, of a perfect life, and was drawn to praise by the splendor of his virtues; but the stream of riches drew him back, and he could not listen to the teaching of the Savior, because he was still thinking of the pleasures of the world. Hence the Savior also speaks: It is difficult for those who have riches to enter the kingdoms of heaven (Matthew 19). And again: No man can serve two masters: for he will either hate the one and love the other; or he is obedient to one and despises the other. You cannot serve God and mammon (Luke 6). But the Pharisees, being greedy, heard these things and laughed at them. We will give up the world, that we may follow the perfect treasure. Those whose souls are possessed by avarice, seem to them a foolish poverty for Christ. There is a great gain in piety with sufficiency. For we brought nothing into this world, nor can we take anything away: for having food and clothing, let us be content with these. But those who want to become rich fall into temptation and a trap, into many lusts, which are foolish and harmful, and men sink into destruction and perdition. For covetousness is the root of all evils (1 Tim. 6).

XXVIII. To this day Elias rebukes Israel, saying: How long will you limp your foot? He is God, go and follow him (3 Kings 18). And he says to us: If these are the commandments of God, which he has delivered to us through our Father, and by following which we can reach the kingdoms of heaven, let us fulfill them with all the same desire. Are we ashamed to be what we are seen to be? Lest it be said to us also: Why have you polluted my holy place (Ezek. 22)? And I will cast them out of my house (Hosea, 9). Indeed, the assembly of the monks is truly the house of God, and the vineyards of the saints, as we read: A vineyard was made for Solomon in a place called Beelamon, he gave it to the keepers, each one brings a thousand pieces of silver for its fruits. My vineyard is in my sight, a thousand for Solomon, and two hundred for those who guard its fruit (Cant. 8). Let us not, therefore, pollute it and throw it away, as we read in the Gospel that those who sold sheep and cattle in it were thrown out of the temple. And the Lord and Savior also entering in, and making himself a scourge of cords, cast them out of the temple, and poured out the brass and the tables of those who sold them, and said to those who sold doves: Take away all these things, and do not make my Father's house a house of merchants. For it is written: My house shall be called a house of prayer to all nations; but you have made it a den of robbers (Luke 19; Mark 11). And elsewhere: Because of you my name is blasphemed among the nations (Ps. 56; Jer. 7).

XXIX. I beseech you, brethren, lest it be said of us also: One is indeed hungry, and another is drunken: has he not houses, that ye may eat and drink? Unless perhaps you despise the Church of God and confound those who have not; to whom it is said: If anyone is hungry, let him eat at home, so that you will not come together for judgment (1 Cor. 11). Let not our house be of a foreign voice, lest it should suit us accordingly: They have not taken away the works of Egypt from themselves. And again: They did not walk in my commandments, and they defiled my sabbaths; therefore, when they cry to me, I will not hear them (Ezek. 20). Let us not continue in hardness of heart, and provoke God to wrath, and let him become our enemy and say: But I will give them precepts that are not good, and justifications in which they do not live (Ibid.); because they ate the fruit of lies, and worshiped the works of their own hands, and their land was filled with augury from the beginning, like the land of strangers.

XXX. Lest after we have renounced the world and begun to follow the standard of the cross, we turn again to the latter, and seek temporal refreshment, imitating Ephraim who said: I have become rich, and I have found refreshment for myself (Hosea xii); let us not hear that which he also deserved to hear: All his labors are not found before the iniquities in which he sinned. And lest it be fulfilled in us: You began with the spirit, and now you have finished with the flesh: have you suffered so much for no reason (Gal. 3)? And he said against us: The law has perished from the priest, and the counsel from the elders; and the hands of the people were loosened, the old men at the gate rested, the chosen ones ceased from their psalms (Ezek. 7). And again, it is said: Because of you my name is blasphemed among the nations (Rom. 2): and the despised institutions of our Father creep into oblivion, and we neglect the mediator of God and the saints through our vice.

TEACHING & DISCUSSION

31 For what fruit, or what sign of God's precepts, is to be found in us, or in what we fulfill the profession we have received? Have we not let go of everything and become subject to avarice, and it is said to us: Whence wars and conflicts (James 4)? Was it not from greed? For because each one seeks his own benefit, not that of his neighbor, Ezekiel, still living to this day, reproves us in prophetic language, saying: There were negations in you. The son dishonors the father, and the father reproaches the son (Ezek. 27). What shall we answer on the day of judgment, or what shall we be able to obtain for our defense at the last time? All these things happened to us, because the priests clapped their hands, and the people loved likewise. Because as the people, so the priest (Jer. 5). Therefore, I will repay him, he says, according to his ways, and I will restore his thoughts to him (Hosea 4).

XXXII. I do not speak these things about all of you, but about those who despise the precepts of their elders; and it was much better for them to be ignorant of the way of righteousness, than to return knowingly from that which was delivered to them by the holy commandment (2 Pet. 2). Jeremiah, lamenting such people, writes: My eyes fail in tears, my belly is troubled, my glory is poured out on the earth, because of the brokenness of the daughter of my people, because the child and suckling failed in the streets of the city. They said to their mothers: Where is the wheat and the wine? when they failed as if wounded in the streets of the city, when they poured their souls into the bosom of their mothers (Thren. 2). We know that God does not desire the strength of a horse, nor is He pleased in the thighs of a man (Ps. 146).

XXXIII. And therefore let us return to the Lord our God, that when we pray, he may hear us, who daily exhorts us to be free and to know him. And elsewhere he says: Return to me, and I will return to you. And again: Return unto me, ye children that go back, and I will rule over you (Jer. 3). Ezekiel is similarly challenged and says: Why are you dying, O house of Israel? I do not want the death of the sinner, but only that he turns from his evil way and live (Ezek. 18). And the Lord, the most merciful and the head of all honor, cries out to us in the Gospel and testifies: Come to me, all you who labor and are heavy laden, and I will restore you. Take my yoke upon you, and learn from me, for I am meek and lowly in heart, and you will find rest for your souls (Matthew 11). Let us consider that the goodness of God challenges us to repentance, and holy men encourage us to salvation. Let us not harden our hearts, nor store up wrath for ourselves in the day of wrath and revelation of the righteous judgment of God, who will render to each one according to his works (Rom. 2); but let us return to the Lord with all our heart, and according to the words of Moses who remembers: If you return to the Lord with all your heart, he will purify your heart and the heart of your seed (Deut. 30).

XXXIV. Let us work like good soldiers of Christ and observe what is written: No one who serves God involves himself in worldly affairs, so that he may please him whom he serves (2 Tim. 2). But if a man competes in a race, he is not crowned unless he competes legitimately. The laboring farmer must first share in his fruits. It is written: All people will go each in his own way. But we will be magnified in the name of the Lord our God; they were hindered and fell, but we arose and were raised (Psal. 19).

XXXV. He who walks in the day does not stumble; But he who walks in the night stumbles, because there is no light in him (John 11). But we, as the Apostle said, are not children of transgression to destruction, but of faith to the gain of the soul (Heb. 10). And elsewhere: All of you, he says, are children of light, and children of God (1 Thess. 3). We are not children of the night, nor of darkness. Therefore, if we are children of the light, we must know the things of the light, and do the fruits of the light in every good work: for that which is manifested is light. If we return to the Lord with our whole heart, and dwell in the precepts of his saints and our Father with a simple heart, we shall abound in every good work. But if we are overcome by the pleasures of the flesh, we shall feel the wall during the day as if in the middle of the night: and we shall not find the way to the city and to our habitation, of which it is said: The soul of those who are hungry and thirsty fails (Psalm 16). because they despised the law delivered to them from God and did not listen to the voice of the prophets: and therefore, they could not reach the promised rest.

XXXVI. Let us watch and be attentive: for if he does not spare the natural, he will not spare us. I do not speak of all, but of the negligent, to whom that lamentation will rightly be applied: Woe to those who have departed from me. They are manifest because they have done wickedly to me, because they have

TEACHING & DISCUSSION

forsaken me, the fountain of living water, and have dug for themselves broken cisterns, which cannot hold water (Jer. 2). And because his judges did not listen, let them hear God saying: I have appointed watchers over you. Hear the sound of the trumpet. And they said: We will not listen (Jer. 2). Whence this unbelief? Was it not because they knew strangers and did not oppose them? The Holy Spirit also speaks elsewhere through the prophet: For I am God, your Lord, who formed the heavens and created the earth; whose hands have laid all the host of heaven, and he has not shown them to you, that you should walk after them (Isaiah 45). This indeed he commanded through Moses, saying: "Do not, when you look up to heaven and see the sun and the moon and the stars and all the ornaments of heaven, be deceived by the error of heaven and worship them" (Deut. 4). I am God who brought you out of the land of Egypt, and you do not know God apart from me, and there is no one who can save you besides me. I am the one who fed you in the desert, in the unfit land, and they were filled with satiety, and their hearts were lifted up (Exodus 20). Therefore, they have forgotten me, and I will give them over to be scattered among all the nations (Jer. 9).

XXXVII. Hearing these things, let us wake up as if from sleep, and make ourselves worthy of the service of the Lord, that he may have mercy and say to us: Call upon me, and I will hear you. For he himself says: He who scattered Israel gathered them together. And elsewhere: I will not do it, says he, according to the wrath of my fury, nor will I leave it so as to destroy Ephraim. And again: I will not punish you forever, nor will I always be angry with you. For the spirit proceeds from me, and everything that breathes I have made. And in the same place he joins and says: I gave them true consolation, peace upon peace to those who were near and far: and the Lord said: I will heal them (Jer. 31). In order that we may fully know his mercy, he teaches us in the speech of Jeremiah, saying: If heaven be lifted up above, and if the floor of the earth be humbled below, I will not repay the nation of Israel for all that they have done (Jer. 3).

XXXVIII. And when the Lord's Savior is so merciful, and challenges us to salvation, let us turn our hearts to him: For it is now the hour for us to awake from sleep; the night passed, but the day drew near; Let us therefore lay aside the works of darkness, and put on the arms of light (Rom. 13). My children, let us first love God with all our hearts, then let us love ourselves one another, remembering the precepts of God the Savior, in which he says: My peace I give you, my peace I leave with you: not as the world gives peace, so I give you. For on these two commandments hangs the whole law, and the prophets (John 14).

XXXIX. If anyone, staying in the house of the monastery under the Superior, is in need of anything that is allowed to be in the monastery, and has a father and a brother and a dearest friend, let him take nothing at all from them, not a coat, not a shawl, not any other thing. But if it is proven that he has less of what are precepts, all fault and correction will be turned to the Prefect.

XL. You, then, who are the leaders of monasteries, if you see them in need of anything, and are appointed to be in distress, do not neglect them, knowing that you will render an account for every flock, over which the Holy Spirit has appointed you to watch over and feed the Church of God, which he acquired with his own blood. (Acts 20). Therefore, we who are stronger ought to bear the infirmities of the weak, and not to please ourselves, but to edify our neighbor in good. For even Christ did not please himself, but as it is written. The reproaches of those who scoffed at you fell upon me (Rom. 15). And again: I do not seek, he says, what is expedient for me, but what is expedient for all, that they may be saved (1 Cor. 20)

XLI. But if the Lord and our Savior so command, and the saints have thus conversed, and our fathers also taught us thus, let us rise from sleep and do what is commanded us. Whatever was written was written for our learning, so that through patience and the consolation of the Scriptures we may have hope (Rom. 15), and none of us should be the cause of another's error, nor should we envy those who do well in their lives. For when they have obtained all that is necessary for the flesh, the dying will take nothing away with them. The children of this world have confidence in this world, because they are of the world, and the world loves what is its own. But those who are children of God, remember the words of the evangelists: If the world hates you, know that it first hated me (John 15). And again: He who wills to be a friend of this world will become an enemy of God. And again: You will have tribulation: but trust me, I have overcome the world. And again: Blessed are they that mourn, for they themselves shall be comforted. Blessed are those who hunger and thirst for

TEACHING & DISCUSSION

righteousness, for they themselves will be satisfied. Blessed are those who suffer persecution for righteousness' sake, for theirs is the kingdom of heaven (Matthew 5). But of the children of the night, what is said on the contrary? Isn't that right? Woe to you, you rich people, because you have received your consolation. Woe to you who are full now, for you will be hungry. Woe to you who laugh now, for you will mourn and weep (Luke 6).

XLII. Wherefore let us shun the friendships of the world, that we may deserve to hear it: Weeping shall be delayed for the evening, and joy for the morning. The Lord heard and had mercy on me. You tore my sack and girded me with joy. For who of the saints has not passed the way of this world in mourning and sorrow? Jeremias: I did not sit down, he said, with the counsel of those playing, but I trembled at the sight of your hand. I sat alone, because I was filled with bitterness (Jer. 15). David also writes: I was humbled as though mourning and mourning (Ps. 34). By standing in their footsteps, we understand that our salvation is in the time of tribulation, and that the promise of the prophet may be fulfilled, saying: Those who are in trouble until the time are not spared. If, therefore, tribulation and distress have a time, and will not be everlasting, let us sow in tears, and reap in joy, not failing; that we know that the Lord delivers his worshipers from temptation.

XLIII. The Lord is our father; The Lord is our judge; The Lord our prince, the Lord our king; The Lord himself will save us; if we neglect his precepts, we shall continue in distress. For he himself says: Those who follow me will possess the earth and inherit my holy mountain (Isaiah 57): which we too will possess if we fulfill his law and hear what is said: Make your ways clean in his sight. And again: Remove the stumbling blocks from the way of my people. And elsewhere: Cast out the pestilence from the council, and strife will go forth with him (Jer. 15). He who calls the just unjust, and the unjust judges the just, both are unclean in the sight of God. Let us beware lest it be said of us also: His children are estranged from him (Psal. 17). And that: The daughters of Zion were exalted, and walked with a high neck, and with the pride of their eyes, dragging their coats with their feet, and playing with their feet together (Isaiah 3), and in our rebuke again the prophetic word agrees, saying: How has the faithful city become a harlot? Zion, full of judgment, in which righteousness sleeps? But now the robbers (Isa. 1). And: The intelligent people mingled with harlots. Therefore, O Israel, do not be ignored (Hosea 4). But if we meditate on the divine, we will be able to say what David did: I will rejoice over your words, as one who finds much spoil (Ps. 118). And: How sweet are your words to my throat, above honey and honeycomb to my mouth. Thy justifications were singable to me in the place of my pilgrimage (Ps. 190). And in another place: I did not set before my eyes an unrighteous thing: I hated those who did iniquity. And my wicked heart did not cleave to me, I did not recognize the evil ones who turned away from me; I pursued him as he drew down in the shadow of his neighbor, with a proud eye and an insatiable heart, while I did not eat at the same time. My eyes are upon the faithful of the earth, that I may make them sit with me.

XLIV. Let us imitate the works of all of them, that there may be peace and justice in our days, and that that which we read elsewhere may not happen to us: On the earth of my people thorns and hay will arise (Isaiah 32). But let us rather invent new things for ourselves, and not sow upon thorns. And when we keep the commandments given to us, it will be evident that we love God, as the divine Scripture testifies in another place: He who hears my commandments and keeps them, it is he who loves me. But he who loves me will be loved by my Father, and I will love him, and I and my Father will come and make our abode with him, and I will show myself to him (John 14). And you are my friends if you do what I command you (John 15). Let us take away many conversations with us, and let us turn to the Lord our God, and let us say to him: You are able to forgive our sins, that we may receive good things, and give him the fruit of our lips (Hosea 14), and our soul may delight in us.

XLV. And may we repent of our error and negligence and turn to our former ways and say: Assyria will not save us; we will not mount upon the horses; and we shall no longer say: Our God is the work of our hands. God, who is in you, will have mercy on the poor, I will heal their dwellings (Hosea 14). And again, he will say of us: I will love them plainly and turn away my wrath from them. I will be like the dew; Israel will blossom like the lily and will send out its roots like Lebanon. Its branches will go away, and it will be like a fruitful olive tree, and its fragrance will be like incense. They shall return, and sit every man in his tents, and shall live, and shall be strengthened with grain: their memory shall blossom as a vineyard, as the fragrance of Ephraim's incense. What about him

TEACHING & DISCUSSION

and the idols? I will humble him and strengthen him. I am like a juniper; from me the fruit thereof was found. Who is wise and understands these things; or does he understand and know these things (Ibid.)? And may we also be able to bear fruit from it, without which no good work can be done.

XLVI. Let us return to the Lord, that he may also say of us: I will remember their sins and their inequities no more (Isaiah 43). Let us not forsake the law of God, which our Father received from him and delivered to us, nor hang on to his little commandments; lest it should be said that he lamented over us: How is the gold darkened, and the good silver unaltered? Nor after the many labors of our Father, which he undertook for our salvation, setting himself an example of virtue, glorying in us, and speaking among the saints. These are my children, and my people are my children, and they will not deny; and after such testimony let us not lose the confidence of a good conscience, stripped of the clothes with which it clothes us; and being introduced by him into the stadium, as we legitimately contend, we shall not be spared by our enemies. And after we have come to that time when we shall depart from the body, lest we become enemies by serving the treasures of our Father: so that we who have had to obtain the freedom of the soul by fasting and affliction of the body, let us devote ourselves to meat and delicacies, and to more beautiful clothes and softer layers, not only by ourselves, but also others who were able to make progress by our example leading to the fall, of whom it is written: You did not receive the spirit of fear of slavery (Rom. 8), but of courage, and of charity, and of chastity. And: Food does not commend us to God. For if we eat, we shall not abound; nor if we do not eat, shall we need. For the kingdom of God is not food and drink, but justice, joy, and peace in the Holy Spirit (Rom. 14). He who serves Christ in this, pleases God, is approved by all. Isaiah also says: Those who wait for the Lord will change their strength, take wings like eagles; they will run and work; they shall march, and shall not hunger (Isaiah 40).
Therefore, he will raise a standard among the nations and gather the refugees of Israel. They will come quickly and quickly: they will not be hungry, nor will they sleep. They shall not sleep, nor loose their belts from their loins, nor break the thongs of their shoes. Whose arrows are sharp, and the bow intent; the feet of horses are like a strong rock: the wheels of chariots are like a storm; they will attack like lions and be present like lion cubs (Ibid. 5).

XLVII. And let us therefore be imitators of the saints and let us not forget the instruction by which our Father taught us while he was still in the body. Let us not put out the burning lamp which he has placed over our heads. As we approach the light of this age, let us remember that through his study God has received us into his own family, giving shelter to strangers, showing us a harbor in stormy seas, bread in famine, shade in heat, clothing in nakedness. he educated the ignorant in spiritual precepts; He surrounded the servants of vice with chastity; He joined them when they were placed at a distance. Let us not forget, after his sleep, so much goodness and immortal benefits, turning wrath into judgment, and the fruit of justice into bitterness, and speaking against us: Judge between me and my vineyard. I waited for it to bear fruit, and it did iniquity, and not justice, but crying (Isa. 5); and let that curse come upon us, which that prophetic word pursues, and which we must flee and avoid with all diligence, following the behavior of those who preceded us in the Lord, Fathers as well as brothers; : how much I fear that we should not lose our laziness, and that prophetic thing is suitable for us, which was said in Ephraim: Oil is traded in Egypt (Hosea 22). They mingled among the nations and learned their works (Psal. 55). Not after we have been called to freedom, as it is written: I will take you one from the people, and two from the family, and will bring you into Zion, and will give you shepherds after my own heart, who will feed you with discipline (Jer. 3); let the bonds of charity be loosed, and let it be said of us: The son glorifies the father, and the servant his master. If I am a father, where is my glory? If the Lord, where is my fear (Malach. 1)?

XLVIII. Therefore each one of us cries out to the Lord: Let the walls of Zion bring down like torrents of tears day and night. Do not give yourself rest, nor let the pupil of your eye be silent. Arise and praise in the night, at the beginning of your watches: pour out your heart like water in the presence of the Lord. Lift up your hands to him for the souls of your little ones who have failed at the head of the world's steps (Thren. 2). Let it not be said against us: The world is bright and corrupt. The high ones of the earth rejoiced, and the earth acted wickedly because of its inhabitants: for they forsook the law, and changed my precepts, the eternal testament. Therefore, a curse will devour the earth, because its inhabitants have sinned and forsaken a few people (Isaiah 24). Lest our wine and vines also mourn, and groan, who formerly rejoiced with all their hearts, and it be said of us: They have confined madness in the house, they are corrupted like the day of the hill. Or that: The capture is from you. And, for you said, we made a covenant with hell and a covenant with death (Isaiah 28). Avoiding these words, we believe more that in due time a star will arise from Jacob and a man will arise from Israel who will strike down the princes of Moab and the sons of Seth (Num. 24). That there may not be in the house of Israel a spur to fury, and a thorn of pain (Ezek. 28). Because Jacob became his portion to the Lord, Israel the cord of his inheritance (Deut. 32). And Jeremiah speaks elsewhere: If this law ceases before me, the nation of Israel may also cease (Jer. 31). And again: I will give their labor to the righteous, and I will make an eternal covenant with them, and their seed and grandchildren will be known among the nations. Everyone who sees them will know that these are the seed blessed by the Lord, and they will enjoy the joys of the Lord (Isaiah 61).

XLIX. And let us therefore scrutinize our ways, and judge our steps, and follow the fragrance of knowledge: always hiding his words in our hearts, that we may be spotless in the way, and walk in the law of the Lord. Let us not be afraid of the frailty of the body, and of the long labors. Where are your fathers, and the Prophets, as it is written, will they live forever? But receive my words and my laws, which I command in my Spirit to my servants the prophets, who were with your fathers (Zech. 1). Let us feel the ineffable mercy of our God, who even today exhorts us to repentance, saying: Shall not he who falls rise again? or he that turneth away, shall not return? Why did my people turn away with the aversion of the shameless, and they prevailed in their pleasures, and would not return (Jer. 8)? If we had returned to him, he would build us with his Spirit, according to what is written: The Lord building Jerusalem, he will gather together the dispersions of Israel (Ps. 146).

L. But that our grouping and communion is from God, by which we join one another, the Apostle taught us, saying: Do not forget the communion of good works, for God is appeased by such victims (Hebrews 13). In the Acts of the Apostles we also read the same thing: But the multitude of believers had one heart and one soul, and no one said anything of his own, but all things were common to them. And with great courage the apostles gave witness to the resurrection of the Lord Jesus (Acts 4). And the Psalmist agreed with the same words, saying: Behold how good and how delightful it is for brothers to dwell together (Ps. 132). And we, dwelling in convents, and united in mutual charity,

TEACHING & DISCUSSION

let us strive, that as we have earned the companionship of the holy Fathers in this life, so we may also be partakers of them in the future: knowing that the cross is the principle of our life and doctrine, and that it is necessary for us to suffer with Christ, and to know that without tribulations and hardships no one can achieve victory. Blessed is the man who suffers temptation, because when he has been tried, he will receive the crown of life (James 4). And again: He labored forever and shall live forever. But if we are pitied, let us be glorified. I consider, he says, that the sufferings of this time are not worthy of the future glory which will be revealed in us (Rom. 8). And elsewhere it is written: I thought, that I might know this, labor is in my sight (Ps. 72). And again: I labored following you and did not consider the day of men (Jer. 17). And in another place: Many are the tribulations of the righteous, and the Lord will deliver them from all these (Ps. 33). And our Lord speaks in the Gospel: He who perseveres to the end will be saved (Matthew 10). And elsewhere: This is a book of commandments, and a law written for ever. All who observe it shall live; but those who forsake them will die. Return, Jacob, and seize him; walk in the splendor of his light, and do not give to another your glory, and those things which they rent to you, to a foreign nation. Blessed are we, O Israel, because the pleas of our God are known to us. Trust, my people, memorable Israel (Baruch. IV). And Isaiah speaks again: Rejoice, O Israel, and celebrate the day, all you who love him. Rejoice, you who trust in him, that you may flee, and be filled from the bosom of his consolation (Isaiah 66).

LI. Let us take care to read and learn the Scriptures, and let us always meditate on them, knowing that it is written: A man shall be satisfied with the fruit of his mouth, and the reward of his lips shall be paid (Prov. 13). These are the things which lead us to the eternal life which our Father has delivered to us and commanded us to constantly meditate on; that that which is written may be fulfilled in us: These words which I command you today shall be in your heart and in your soul; you shall teach them to your children, and speak in them while sitting in the house, and walking on the road, and lying down, and rising. Write them for a sign in your hand, and they shall be immovable before your eyes. You shall also write them on the posts of your houses, and on the thresholds, so that you may learn to fear the Lord all the days that you live (Deut. 11). Solomon also, signifying himself, says: Write them in the breadth of your heart (Prov. 3).

TEACHING & DISCUSSION

LI. Consider how many testimonies the word of the Lord exhorts us to meditate on the sacred Scriptures, so that what we speak with our mouth we may possess with our heart. It is good for a man when he has lifted the yoke from his youth. He will sit alone and be silent, because he will lift the yoke on himself, he will give his cheek to the one who strikes, he will be satiated with insults, because the Lord will not always cast him off (Thren. 3). And elsewhere it is written: I am reminded of the mercies of your childhood. And again: Rejoice, young man, in your youth, and let your heart rejoice in the days of your youth and walk in the ways of your heart without spot, and in the sight of your eyes, and know that in all these the Lord will bring you in judgment. Remove anger from your heart and malice from your flesh, because youth and foolishness are vanity (Eccl. 11). And remember your creator in the days of your youth, until the worst days come and occupy the years in which you will say: I have no will in them; until the sun, and the light, and the moon, and the stars are darkened, and the clouds turn after the rain. In the day when the guardians of the house shall be moved, and the men of valor shall be overthrown, and the laborers shall cease, because few things have been done; and they will be darkened by what they see in the holes, and they will close the roads in the marketplace in the weakness of the voice of the grinding. And they shall arise at the voice of the sparrow, and all the children of song shall be humbled. And indeed, they will look from a height, and the terrors on the road, and the almond blossoms, and the locusts grow fat, and the capers are split. For a man has gone to the house of his age, and those who mourn go round in the market-place, until the silver cord is broken, and the gold necklace is broken, and the jar is broken at the fountain, and the wheel is hindered over the lake, and the dust is turned to the ground, as it was, and the spirit returns to the Lord, who gave him (Ibid. 12). It is also written in the Gospel: Children, do you have any soup? Cast to the right side of the ship, and you will find them (John 21). And again: Every child and young man who does not know good and evil today will themselves enter the good land. And again: Every male that opens the womb shall be called holy (Exodus 15). And in the Gospel: And the child went, and grew, and prospered with God and with men (Luke 2). Jesus, too, was a young servant of Moses, and did not go out of the tabernacle of God. And we read what is written about David: A boy of yellow color, with elegant eyes (1 Kings 16). Timothy, too, while still a child and a youth, was educated in the sacred letters, in order to arrive at the faith of the Lord and Savior by those paths. And of Daniel, because he was learned, we read that he was called a man of desires (Dan. 10). Joseph was also very dear to his father, because he served his orders, and when he was still seventeen years old he considered his precepts to be the law of his life.

LIII. And I repeated all this, so that considering the lives of the saints, we should not be carried about by every wind of doctrine (Eph. 4) but let us work hard and let their behavior be the purpose of our lives as an example, so that we may be God's special people. Nor let us grieve the Holy Spirit, in whom we were sealed on the day of redemption; let us not extinguish it in ourselves: and let us not despise the prophecies; lest perhaps we give place to the Holy Spirit willing to dwell in us. Let us fear no one else, except God, who is the avenger and judge of individual deeds, and is holy with the holy, and innocent with the innocent man (Ps. 17). and he says: I love those who love me, and those who seek me will find joy (Prov. 8). And elsewhere he says: If you walk against me perversely, I will walk perversely against you (Lev. 26).

LIV Let us not be angry with one another (Psal. 4): even if anger overcomes us, let us not sin in anger, preoccupied with penitence after falling asleep (Matt. 18). Let us remember that it is a commandment, whenever we are to forgive those who sin against us, and to leave our offering before the altar: which is by no means accepted, if it is not appeased by reconciliation (Ibid. 5): so that we may say: Forgive us our debts, as we also forgive our debtors (Luke 11). And the apostle commanded: If anyone has a complaint against anyone, just as Christ also gave us, do the same (Col. 5). Let us be disciples of the meekness of all the saints, and especially of David, of whom it is written: Remember, O Lord, David, and all his meekness (Ps. 211). And Moses, of whom it is read, that he was meek over all the earth (Num. 12). And the Lord speaks in the Gospel about the meek and the meek: Blessed are the meek and meek in heart, for they will inherit the earth (Matthew 5). It is of great wisdom to possess meekness, and to hear: Be wise, my son, that my heart may rejoice (Prov. 10). And again: Be imitators of God, beloved children (Eph. 5). And be perfect, even as your Father who is in heaven is perfect (Mark 5). And elsewhere: Be holy, because I am holy, says the Lord (Lev. 5).

TEACHING & DISCUSSION

LV. Having read these testimonies, let us sow righteousness for ourselves, that we may reap the fruit of life. Let us shine the light of knowledge, because it is time for us to know God, until the fruits of righteousness come to us. Behold, now is the acceptable time, and the day of salvation (2 Cor. 6). And truly, according to what is written, the fullness of the law is love (Rom. 13). John in this same context: We have received this commandment from the Father, that you love one another (John 15). And he that loveth God, let him also love his brother (2 John 4). And, not like Cain, who was of evil origin, killed his brother. And why did he kill? because his works were evil; and his brother's goods. Let us not be surprised, brothers, if the world hates us: we know ourselves, because we have passed from death to life, because we love our brothers (1 John 3). Therefore, let us love one another.

LVI. I will speak to you more boldly, dearest children. From the time that God entrusted to me the flock of your conversation and holy conversation, I have not ceased to admonish with tears, and to teach each one, that you may please God; nor did I take away anything that I felt was useful to you, so as to say: And now I commend you to God, and to the word of his grace, who is able to build you up and give you an inheritance with the saints (Acts 20). Watch, strive with all diligence and care, lest you forget your purpose, but fulfill what you know to have been promised. For I am already erased, and the time of my resolution is at hand: I have fought the good fight in part, I have finished the course, I have kept the faith. Of the rest, there is laid up for me the crown of righteousness, which the Lord will give me on that day as a just judge: not only to me, but also to all who loved his righteousness (2 Tim. 4) and did all the commandments of the Father. The end of the word: hear everything, fear God and keep his commandments; for every man: God will bring the whole work into judgment, whether it be good or bad (Eccl. 12). The doctrine of St. Orsisius is explicit.

TEACHING & DISCUSSION

LATIN TEXT

Doctrina atque tractatus

I. Audi, Israel, mandata vitae; auribus percipe, et intellige prudentiam. Quid est, Israel, quod in terra inimicorum es? Inveterasti in terra aliena; commaculatus es cum mortuis; comparatus es cum his qui in inferno sunt, et dereliquisti fontem sapientiae. Per viam Dei si ambulasses, forsitan habitaveris in pace. Disce ergo, ait, ubi est prudentia tua, ubi est fortitudo gloriae atque virtutis, ubi est intelligentia, ubi lex oculorum, et pax. Qui invenit locum ejus, et quis ingressus est ad thesauros illius (Bar. III)? Haec loquebatur Baruch propter eos qui in terram Babylonis et inimicorum suorum ducti sunt in captivitatem, quia noluerunt prophetarum suscipere mandata, et obliti sunt legis Dei, quae data est per Moysen. Idcirco induxit Deus super eos poenas atque supplicia, et captivitatis subdidit jugo: erudiens ergo eos ut suos, et quasi pater filios emendans, nolensque perire correctos, sed salvare cupiens per poenitentiam.

II. Unde et nos apostolicorum debemus meminisse verborum, qui ait: Si naturatibus ramis non pepercit, nec nobis parcet (Rom. XI), et Dei praecepta complere negligimus? Haec omnia in figuris contingebant illis: scripta sunt autem ad correptionem nostram, in quos fines saeculorum devenerunt (I Cor. X). Et illi quidem de urbe Judae translati sunt in urbem Chaldaeorum, in terris mutantes loca: nos autem si Deus viderit negligentes, in futuro saeculo amittemus civitatem nostram; et laetitiam deserentes, trademus poenarum captivitati, perdemusque gaudium sempiternum, quod patres nostri et fratres labore instabili repererunt.

III. Igitur non nos vincat oblivio, nec patientiam Dei existimemus ignorantiam, qui idcirco sustenta et differt, ut ad meliora conversi cruciatibus non tradamur. Quando peccamus, non putemus Deum consentire nostris peccatis, quia non statim vindicat; sed illud cogitemus, quod cito exeuntes de saeculo separabimur in futuro a Patribus et fratribus nostris, qui locum victoriae possident. Quem et nos habebimus, si illorum voluerimus calcare vestigia, et illud attendere, quod apostolus Paulus hic quoque sanctos a peccatoribus separat, et tradit delinquentes in interitum carnis, ut spiritus salvus fiat (I Cor. V). Beatus homo qui timet Dominum, et quem corripit ut emendetur, et legem suam docet eum, ut ambulet in mandatis ejus omnibus diebus vitae suae; qui non murmurat pro peccato suo.

IV. Itaque et nos scrutemur vias nostras, et gressus proprios dijudicemus; revertamurque ad Dominum, et levemus cum manibus nostris corda nostra in excelsum et in coelum: ut in die judicii adjutor noster sit, et non confundamur cum loquimur inimicis nostris in porta, sed magis digni simus illud audire: Aperite portas, ut ingrediatur populus qui custodit justitiam et veritatem (Judit. XV). Cui veritas cordi est, et qui possidet pacem, dicere potest: Quia in te speravimus, Domine, in aeternum. Recordemur Domini, et Hierusalem ascendat super cor nostrum. Ne obliviscamur illius hominis, de quo scriptum est: Benedictus homo qui confidit in Domino, cujus est spes in eo. Erit quasi lignum fructiferum juxta aquas, et ad humorem mittit radices suas: non timebit, cum aestus advenerit, habebitque frondentes ramos, et in tempore siccitatis virebit, poma sollicita germinans. Grave cor in omnibus, et homo est, et quis cognoscit eum? Ergo Dominus scrutans corda et renes, ut reddam unicuique secundum vias suas (Jer. XVII).

V. Meminerimus nostri, nec contemnamus delicta quae fecimus; et singula mandata Patris nostri et eorum qui nos docuerunt, corde sollicito pertractemus: non solum credentes in Christo, sed et pro ipso patientes, et scientes illud de quo dicitur: Spiritus vultus nostri Christus Dominus (Thren. IV). Et alibi: Lucerna pedibus meis lex tua, et lumen semitis meis. Et iterum: Eloquium Domini vivificavit me, et, Lex Domini immaculata, convertens animas. Mandatum Domini lucidum, illuminans oculos (Psalm. CXVIII). Et Apostolus, Lex, inquit, sancta, et mandatum sanctum, et justum, et bonum (Rom. VII). Quae omnia intelligentes, digni erimus audire: Cum ceciderit justus non allidetur, quia Dominus sustentat manum illius (Psalm. XXXVI). Et iterum: Septies cadet justus, et resurget (I Petr. III).

VI. Nunc ergo, fratres, Deo agente patienter, et nos ad poenitentiam provocante, de gravi somno evigilemus, quia adversarius noster quasi leo rugiens circuit quaerens quem devoret (I Petr. V), cui acriter resistendum est, et sciendum eadem etiam certamina nostris evenisse majoribus. Non deficiamus laborantes jacientesque virtutum semina, ut in futuro gaudia metere possimus, audiamusque Paulum docentem: Tu autem qui servasti doctrinam, eruditionem, studium, patientiam, persecutionem, et sanctorum exempla sectantes permaneamus in eo quod coepimus, habentes principem et perfectorem Jesum. Intelligamus comam capitis nostri in via, ut sit unguentum in barba nostra, ut ad oram perveniat vestimenti, ut possimus implere universa, quae scripta sunt (Psalm. CXXXII).

VII. Quapropter, o duces et praepositi monasteriorum ac domorum, quibus crediti sunt homines, et apud quos inveniuntur T, sive E, sive A, ut in commune dicam, quibus crediti sunt homines, singuli cum turmis suis exspectent Salvatoris adventum, ut conspectui illius ornatum armis exercitum praeparent. Ne refrigeretis eos in carnalibus, et spiritalia non tribuatis alimenta. Aut rursum doceatis spiritalia, et in carnalibus affligatis, in escis videlicet atque vestitu. Sed et spiritales et carnales cibos pariter tribuite, et nullam detis eis occasionem negligentiae. Aut quae est ista justitia, ut fratres labore affligamus, et ipsi otio vacemus? aut eis jugum imponamus, quod ipsi ferre non possumus. Legimus in Evangelio: Qua mensura mensi fueritis remetietur vobis (Matth. VII). Unde et laborem et refrigeria cum ipsis habeamus communia, nec discipulos servos putemus, et illorum tribulatio sit nostra laetitia; ne evangelicus nos cum Pharisaeis corripiat: Vae vobis legisperitis, qui ligatis onera importabilia, et imponitis ea super humeros hominum, et ipsi ne digito quidem audetis attingere (Matth. XXIII).

VIII. Sunt aliqui attendentes semetipsos, ut viventes juxta mandatum Dei sibi loquuntur, et dicunt: Quid mihi est cum aliis? Ego vero ut serviam Deo, et mandata ejus impleam, non ad me pertinet quid alii faciant. Hoc Ezechiel corripit dicens: O pastores Israel, nunquid semetipsos pascunt pastores? nonne oves pascunt? Ecce lac comedistis, et lanis operimini, quod pingue est non immolastis, et quod infirmum est non confortastis; quod fractum est non ligastis; quod errabat non reduxistis; quod perierat non quaesistis; quod forte erat fecistis labore deficere, et dispersistis oves meas, eo quod non haberent pastores (Ezech. XXXIV). Propterea ipse Dominus veniet cum senioribus et principibus suis, et complebitur illud in nobis: Exactores vestri depraedantur vos, et qui repetunt, errare vos faciunt (Isai. III). Quin magis audire debemus: Beata terra, cujus rex filius: ingenui et principes tui in tempore comedunt in fortitudine, et non confundentur (Eccl. X).

IX. Ideo, o homo, usque ad unam animam, quae tibi credita est, monere non cesses et docere quae sancta sunt, et teipsum bonorum operum praebere exemplum, et cavere quam maxime, ne alterum ames et alterum oderis, sed et cunctis exhibeas aequalitatem: ne forte quem tu diligis Deus oderit, et quem tu oderis Deus diligat. Nulli erranti pro amicitia consentias, et alterum premas, et alterum subleves, et pereat labor tuus. Sedentes in locis humilioribus, in quibus Pater noster praecipit penitus non sedendum, caveant praepositi domorum, ne forsitan quilibet unus ex fratribus praeposito injuriam fecerit, et iratus ille discernat ac dicat: Quid causae habeo ad hominem contemptorem? Faciat quod vult, ad me non pertinet; nec eum moneo, nec errantem corrigo, sive salvetur, sive pereat, ad me non pertinet. O homo, quid haec loqueris? Intellige quo furore supereris et odium occupavit cor tuum, ut magis tuo vitio quam suo peccato frater pereat; cui debes ignoscere, et eum suscipere poenitentem, ut possis illud evangelicum dicere: Dimitte nobis debita nostra, sicut et nos dimittimus debitoribus nostris (Matth. VI). Si ergo vis ut Deus peccata tua tibi dimittat, et tu dimitte fratri tuo quidquid illud est quod in te peccavit, memor illius praecepti: Ne oderis fratrem tuum in corde tuo (Luc. XI). Et Salomonis monentis: Suscita civem tuum pro quo spopondisti (Prov. VI). Et iterum: Ne cesses erudire parvulum, si enim virga percusseris eum, non morietur (Prov. XXIII). Moysen quoque ausculta dicentem: Correptione corripies proximum tuum, ne habeas peccatum pro eo (Levit. XIX). Ne eveniat rursum illud Salomonis: Qui non praedicit filio, ut se custodiat a perditionibus, velociter dissolvetur (Prov. XIX).

X. Omnes quibus fratrum cura commissa est, parent se adventui Salvatoris et formidoloso tribunali ejus. Si enim pro se ipso reddere rationem plenum est discriminis ac timoris, et quanto magis pro alterius culpa subire cruciatum, et incidere in manus Dei viventis? Nec possumus obtendere ignorantiam, cum scriptum sit: Omne factum Deus adducet in judicio, in omnibus quae neglecta sunt, sive bonum, sive malum (Eccl. XII). Et in Apostolo legimus: Omnes nos oportet manifestari ante tribunal Christi, ut unusquisque recipiat pro eo quod operatus est, sive bonum, sive malum (II Cor. V). Isaias quoque diem constitutam significat, in qua judicaturus sit Deus orbem terrae in justitia, dicens: Ecce dies Domini insanabilis venit furoris et irae, ut ponat orbem terrae in deserto, et perdat peccatores de eo (Isai. III). Scimus quia omnia quae in lege scripta sunt, et prophetarum nobis vaticinia praedixerunt, sanctus quoque

TEACHING & DISCUSSION

Pater noster erudivit, nos esse retinendos et reddituros rationem de singulis, quare non fecerimus ea, aut negligentius fecerimus. Loquitur enim cui traditum est a Patre omne judicium, et veritas erudit veritatem: Non putetis quia ego accuso vos ad Patrem; est qui vos accuset Moyses, in quo vos speratis. Si enim crederetis Moysi, crederetis et mihi: de me enim ille scripsit (Joan. IV).

XI. Ex quibus omnibus discimus, quod oporteat nos stare ante tribunal Christi, et de singulis non solum operibus, sed et cogitationibus judicari: et post rationem vitae nostrae, etiam pro aliis qui nobis crediti sint reddituros esse similiter rationem. Et hoc non solum de Praepositis domorum audiendum est, sed et de monasteriorum principibus, et de singulis fratribus qui reputantur in plebem: quia omnes invicem debent sua onera portare, ut adimpleant legem Christi (Gal. VI), et audiant Apostolum scribentem ad Timotheum: O Timothee, depositum custodi, devitans profanas vocum novitates, et professionem falsi nominis scientiae (I Tim. VI). Et nos habemus depositum a Deo traditum, conversatione fratrum, pro quibus laborantes et exspectamus futura praemia: ne forsitan dicatur et nobis: Dimitte populum istum, ut abeat (Exod. V); et traditiones Patris nostri deserentibus ingeratur: Qui habent legem non noverunt me, pastores egerunt impie in me (Jer. II). Unde alios corripit dicens: Ego dedi haereditatem meam in manu tua, tu autem non dedisti ullam misericordiam: senes aggravasti jugo (Isai. XLVII). Quod et nos non solum audire, verum etiam intelligere necesse est: qui enim ignorat ignorabitur. Et in alio loco scriptum est: Quia tu scientiam meam repulisti, et ego repellam te, ne sacerdotio fungaris mihi (Oseae IV).

XII. Itaque, fratres charissimi, qui coenobiorum vitam et praecepta sectamini, state in arrepto semel proposito, et implete opus Dei, ut Pater, qui primus instituit coenobia gaudens pro nobis loquatur ad Dominum: Sicut tradidi eis, sic vivunt. Quod idem et Apostolus adhuc in corpore constitutus loquebatur: Laudo autem vos, quod in omnibus meministis mei, et sicut tradidi vobis traditiones meas custodistis (I Cor. XI).

XIII. Et vos ergo monasteriorum principes, esstote solliciti, et adhibete omnem curam pro fratribus cum timore et justitia Dei: nec abutamini potestate in supplicia, sed exemplum praebete vos cunctis et subdito gregi; sicut et

Dominus noster in omnibus exemplum se praebuit, qui posuit quasi oves familias: ut misereamini gregi vobis credito, et memineritis apostolicae sententiae, in qua ait: Nihil subtraxi, ut non annuntiarem vobis omnem voluntatem Dei. Et iterum: Non cessavi deprecando unumquemque vestrum, et docendo vos publice (Act. XX). Videte quanta viscera et quanta misericordia fuerint in homine Dei, qui non solum sollicitus est pro omnibus ecclesiis, sed languet cum languentibus, et omnium sustinet passiones. Caveamus, ne per nostram negligentiam aliquis scandalizetur, et corruat, et obliviscamur verborum Domini Salvatoris, qui in Evangelio loquitur: Pater, quos dedisti mihi, non perdidi ex eis quemquam (Joan. XVII). Nullam animam contemnamus, ne quisque per nostram duritiem pereat. Si enim aliquis propter nos fuerit mortuus, anima nostra pro illius anima tenebitur in reatu. Quod quidem et Pater noster indesinenter nobis solebat inculcare, et monebat, ne illud eloquium impleretur in nobis: Singuli opprimunt proximum suum: et iterum: Si invicem mordetis et devoratis, videte ne adinvicem consumamini (Gal. V). Ex quo apparet quod qui alterius servat animam, custos animae suae sit.

XIV. Sed et vos qui secundi estis monasterii, primos vos exhibete virtutibus, ne quis vitio vestro pereat. Ne incurratis in illud opprobrium in quod incurrit ille qui comedit et bibit cum ebriis, et non dedit in tempore suo conservis cibaria: Et veniet Dominus in die qua non sperat, et in hora qua nescit, ut dividat eum, et ponat partem ejus cum hypocritis, ubi fletus et stridor est dentium (Matth. XXIV). Ne quos apprehendat e vobis similis condemnatio, sed cum tempora venerint refrigerii mereamur audire: Euge, serve bone et fidelis: quia super modicum fuisti fidelis, supra multa te constituam, intra in gaudium Domini tui (Luc. XIX). XV. Vos quoque Praepositi domorum singularum, parati estote ad respondendum omnibus qui a vobis exigunt rationem super ea fide quae in vobis est. Monete eos qui inordinati sunt; consolamini pusillanimes; sustinete infirmos; patienter agite ad omnes, et audite Apostolum monentem: Et, vos patres, nolite ad iram provocare filios vestros, sed enutrite illos in disciplina et admonitione Domini (Ephes. VI), et scitote quia cui plus datum est, plus quaeretur ab eo; et cui plus creditum est, amplius exigetur (Luc. XII). Nec tantum ea consideretis, quae vobis prosint, sed illa quae proximis, et impleatur in vobis Scriptura dicens: Quia vos sequimini unusquisque utilitatem domus suae, idcirco continebit coelum rorem suum, et terra non dabit fructus suos,

TEACHING & DISCUSSION

quoniam ingravastis contra me sermones vestros (Reg. I). Dicitur et alibi: Quia non fecistis uni ex minimis, nec mihi fecistis (Matth. XXV).

XVI. Saepius dicam, et eadem repetam: Cavete ne alios diligatis, et alios oderitis; ne hunc sustentetis, et illum negligatis; et cassus inveniatur labor vester, et omnis sudor pereat; et quando exieritis de corpore et de mundi hujus turbine liberati, portum vos putaveritis quietis intrare; tunc inveniatis injustitiae naufragia, et in qua mensura mensi estis, remetiatur vobis ab eo qui personas in judicio non accipit. Si quid mortale, aut aliquid turpitudinis ob negligentiam Praepositorum in domibus commissum fuerit, post illorum propria supplicia, Praepositus quoque reus tenebitur criminis: quod nobis semper sanctae memoriae Pater noster solebat ingerere.

XVII. Quamobrem cum omni cautione et sollicitudine singuli commissum sibi gregem custodiant, et imitentur pastores de Evangelio, ad quos non dormientes, sed vigilantes venit Angelus Dei, et Salvatoris eis annuntiavit adventum (Luc. II). Qui et ipse loquitur: Pastor bonus animam suam ponit pro ovibus suis: qui autem mercenarius est, non est pastor, cujus non sunt oves, videt lupum venientem, et dimittit gregem, et fugit, et lupus rapit eum, atque devastat, quia mercenarius est, et non ad eum pertinet de ovibus (Joan. XII). De bonis autem pastoribus Lucae scribit historia: Erant autem pastores observantes, et custodientes vigilias noctis super gregem suum; et angelus Domini venit ad eos, et gloria Dei circumfulsit eos, et timuerunt timore magno; dixitque eis angelus: Nolite timere: ecce enim evangelizo vobis gaudium magnum, quod erit omni populo: quia est hodie vobis natus Salvator, qui est Christus Dominus in civitate David. Et hujus rei signum erit vobis, invenietis infantem pannis involutum et positum in praesepio (Luc. II). Num illi soli eo tempore pascebant oves, et per desertum sequebantur gregem? Sed quia soli erant solliciti, et naturalem noctium somnum insidiantium luporum timor superabat, idcirco primi audire meruerunt, quod in vicino sit: at Hierosolyma dormiens ignorabat. Unde et David dicit: Ecce non dormiet, qui custodit Israel (Psal. LXX). Itaque et vos cum tremore et timore vigilate, operantes vestram salutem, et scientes quod universitatis Dominus, per quem omnis caro receptura est quidquid operata est, post resurrectionem solis apostolis apparuit, et dixit apostolorum principi, Petro: Simon Joannis, diligis me plus his? Respondit ei: Domine, tu scis quia ego diligo te. Dicit ei Jesus: Pasce agnos meos. Dicit ei rursum secundo: Simon Joannis, diligis me? Respondit ei: Etiam, Domine, tu scis quia diligam te. Dicit ei: Pasce oves meas (Joan. XXI). Tertio praecepit ut pasceret oves: et in illo omnibus nobis hoc injunxit officium, ut diligenter pascamus oves Domini, et in die visitationis ejus pro labore ac custodia recipiamus, quae nobis in Evangelio promisit dicens? Pater, volo ut ibi sum ego, et isti sint mecum. Et iterum: Ubi ego sum, ubi et minister meus erit (Joan. XII). Respiciamus ad promissa et ad praemia creduli, facilius omnem perferamus laborem, ambulantes sicut ambulavit ipse Dominus, qui promissor est praemiorum.

XVIII. Vos quoque qui secundi estis singularum domorum, humilitatem sectamini et modestiam, et singula praecepta majorum vitae communis normam putate, ut in illis conservandis vestras servetis animas, et similes sitis ei qui ait: Anima mea in manibus meis semper (Psal. CXVIII). Filius glorificet Patrem, et laetamini fructibus vestris: quia absque operibus et fructibus nullus Domini societate laetabitur: ut cum habueritis fructum in Domino, ipso haerede et cohaerede potiamini.

XIX. Sed et vos omnes fratres, qui subjecti estis per ordinem liberae servitutis, habetote accinctos lumbos vestros, et ardentes lucernas in manibus, similes servorum qui exspectant dominum suum, quando revertatur de nuptiis, ut cum venerit, et pulsaverit, statim aperiant ei. Beati servi, quos veniens Dominus invenerit vigilantes (Luc. XI). Sic et vobis fiet, si longus labor lassitudinem non operetur in vobis, vocabimini ad coeleste convivium et angeli ministrabunt vobis. Hae sunt repromissiones custodientium mandata Dei, et ista praemia futurorum, Gaudete in Domino; rursum dico, gaudete (Phil. IV). Subjecti Patribus cum omni obedientia; sine murmurationibus, et cogitationibus variis, simplicitatem animae ad bona opera perferentes, ut pleni virtutibus et timore Dei, digni efficiamini adoptione Dei. Arripite scutum fidei, in quo possitis omnes sagittas diaboli ardentes restinguere, et gladium Spiritus, quod est verbum Dei (Ephes. VI). Estote prudentes sicut serpentes, et simplices sicut columbae (Matth. X). Audite Paulum loquentem: Filii, obedite parentibus (Col. III), et possidete salutem animarum vestrarum, per eos qui vobis praepositi sunt. Et in alio quoque loco scriptum est: Acquiescite principibus vestris et subjicimini, quia ipsi vigilant pro animabus vestris, rationem reddentes pro vobis (I Cor. III). Et semper illud timete, quod idem Apostolus loquitur: Templum Dei estis, et Spiritus Domini habitat in vobis. Si quis autem templum Dei violaverit, disperdet illum Deus (Ephes. IV). Et iterum: Nolite contristare Spiritum sanctum Dei, in quo signati estis in diem redemptionis justi judicii (Ibid.).

XX. Servate pudicitiam corporis vestri, ut sitis hortus conclusus, fons signatus (Cant. VI). Qui enim natus ex Deo non peccat, quoniam semen illius in eo permanet (I Joan. III). Idem Joannes loquitur: Scribo vobis, juvenes, quoniam fortes estis, et sermo Dei in vobis permanet, et vicistis malignum (I Joan. II). Cum et vos viceritis inimicum, Deo vobis praebente auxilium, tunc et ipse dicet: Eruam eos de inferno, et redimam eos de morte. Ubi est, mors, contentio tua? ubi est, mors, stimulus tuus (Oseae, XIII)? Si vero mortem devorabimus, superabimus eam, et dicetur nobis: Mors ei nequaquam dominabitur (Rom. VI): quoniam mors, qua peccato mortui semel sumus, in nobis mortua est, et vita, qua in Christo vivimus, semper vivimus (Rom. VII). Qui enim in carne moritur, justificabitur a peccato. Nequaquam ultra vivamus in desideriis hominum, sed reliquam vitam in voluntate Dei expleamus. Qui timetis Dominum armate vos castitate, ut audire mereamini: Vos autem non estis in carne, sed in spiritu (Ibid.). Et scitote quod perfectis perfecta tribuantur, et inanibus reddantur inania, juxta sermonem Evangelicum: Qui habet, dabitur ei, et abundabit; qui autem non habet, et quod videbatur habere, auferetur ab eo (Marc. IV). Imitemur virgines sapientes, quae cum sponso thalamum ingredi meruerunt, quae habebant in vasis suis et lampadibus oleum bonorum operum. Porro stultae virgines clausam thalami januam repererunt, quia ante nuptias parare sibi oleum noluerunt (Matth. XXV). Haec in figura contingebant illis; scripta sunt enim ad correctionem nostram (I Cor. X), ut evitemus vetera, et servemus praecepta sapientis, qui ait: Fili mi, si sapiens fuerit cor tuum, laetificabis cor meum, et commemorabunt labia mea sermones tuos (Prov. XXIII), si tamen recti fuerint. Et iterum: Non aemuletur cor tuum peccatores, sed in timore Dei esto tota die, et Dei cultum observa jugiter (Prov. XXIII).

XXI. Vigilemus attentius, et sciamus quod magnam nobis Deus praestiterit gratiam per Patrem nostrum Pachomium, ut renuntiaremus saeculo; et omnem sollicitudinem mundi, et curas rerum saecularium pro nihilo poneremus. Quae nobis occasio relicta est, ut habeamus quidquam proprium a funiculo usque ad corrigendum calceamenti; cum habeamus Praepositos, qui pro nobis cum timore et tremore solliciti sunt tam in cibo, et vestitu, et corpusculi languore, si forte obvenerit, ut in nullo timeamus, et per occasionem carnis animae emolumenta perdamus? Liberi sumus, jugum de cervicibus nostris mundanae servitutis abjecimus; cur rursum volumus reverti ad vomitum nostrum, et aliquid habere unde solliciti simus, et quod perdere metuamus? Ad quos usus superfluum palliolum, aut epulae lautiores, aut melior lectus? cum omnia in commune sint praeparata, et nihil cruce Christi durius sit, juxta quam viventes Patres nostri aedificaverunt nos super fundamentum apostolorum et prophetarum, et evangeliorum disciplinam, quae angulari continetur lapide Domino Jesu Christo (Ephes. II): quem sequentes de mortifera altitudine ad vitalem descendimus humilitatem, divitias paupertate mutantes, et delicias simplici cibo. XXII. Nolite, obsecro vos, oblivisci semel arrepti propositi, et traditiones Patris nostri scalas putemus ad coelorum regna tendentes. Ne desideretis quae ante calcastis. Sufficit nobis habere, quod homini satis est, duo levitonaria, et alium attritum, et palliolum lineum, duos cucullos, zonam lineam, gallicas, pellem, et virgam. Cui ministerium aliquod et dispensatio est credita monasterii, et si ex ea lucrum faciat, scelus putetur, et sacrilegium quidquam ex ea contingere et in propriam vertere requiem, quasi despiciens eos qui non habent et felici paupertate sunt divites: ut non solum ipse perierit, sed et caeteros provocet ad pereundum. Et illi quidem qui incurvaverunt cervicem suam, et cum omni humilitate et afflictione lugentes atque plangentes in praesentiarum placuerunt Deo, cum de corpusculo isto exierint, ducentur, et accumbent cum sanctis patribus Abraham, Isaac, et Jacob, prophetis, et apostolis, et consolatione digna fruentur, sicut et Lazarus fruitus est in sinu Abraham. Qui autem vixerunt in coenobio, et de communi in suos aliquid averterunt usus, vae eis cum de corpore exieriat, dicetur illis: Mementote, quia recepistis bona in vita vestra (Luc. XVI); fratribus laborantibus, et jejuniis et continentia, et incessabili labore sudantibus. Idcirco videte eos in gaudio atque laetitia, qui reliquerunt praesentem vitam, ut futuram consequerentur: vos autem in squalore ac tormentis, et miseria constitutos, quia noluistis evangelicum audire sermonem, et Isaiae contempsistis verba dicentis: Ecce qui serviunt mihi, comedent, vos autem esurietis. Ecce qui serviunt mihi, bibent, vos autem sitietis. Ecce qui serviunt mihi, exsultabunt, et vos clamabitis propter dolorem cordis vestri, et ob contritionem spiritus ejulabitis (Isai. LXV). Audistis omnes beatitudines Scripturarum, et noluistis suscipere disciplinam.

TEACHING & DISCUSSION

XXIII. Ideo, fratres, aequales simus, a minimo usque ad maximum, tam dives quam pauper, concordia et humilitate perfecti, ut de vobis quoque possit dici: Qui multum, non abundavit; qui parum, non indiguit (II Cor. VIII). Ne quis suis provideat deliciis, cernens fratrem in paupertate et angustia constitutum, et dicatur ei illud propheticum: Nonne Deus unus creavit vos? Nonne Pater unus omnium vestrum? Quare dereliquistis unusquisque fratrem suum, ut abominabile facerent testamentum patrum vestrorum? Derelictus est Juda, sed abominatio facta est in Israel (Malac. II). Quapropter juxta illud quod Dominus atque Salvator praecepit apostolis dicens: Mandatum novum do vobis, ut diligatis invicem, sicut et ego dilexi vos: et in hoc scietis, quod vere discipuli mei estis (Joan. XIII); nos invicem amare debemus, et ostendere, quod vere simus famuli Domini Jesu Christi, et filii Pachomii, et discipuli coenobiorum.

XXIV. Si Praepositus domus aliquem corripuerit ex fratribus qui sibi subjecti sunt, erudiens eum in timore Dei et cupiens ab errore corrigere, et alius voluerit pro eo loqui, et eum defendere, subvertens cor illius; qui hoc facit, peccat in suam animam, quia subvertit eum qui corrigi poterat, et consurgentem dejicit in terram, atque ad meliora tendentem mala persuasione decepit, errans ipse, et alios errare faciens. Huic illud aptabitur congruenter: Vae qui potum dat proximo suo subversionem turbidam, et inebrians eum (Habac. II). Vae qui errare facit caecum in via (Deut. XXVII). Qui scandalizat quempiam de his, qui credunt Deo, expedit ei ut appendatur ei mola asinaria super collum ejus, et praecipitetur in mare (Matth. XVIII). Quia subvertit, ut diximus, sublevantem se, et obedientem transtulit ad superbiam, et eum qui in dulcedine charitatis poterat ambulare, convertit in amaritudinem; et subjectum legibus monasterii, malis consiliis depravavit, fecitque odisse eum, et contristari contra illum, qui eum docebat Domini disciplinam, lites ferens inter fratres atque discordias, et non timens illud quod scriptum est: Tu quis es, qui judicas alienum serrum? Suo domino stat, aut cadit. Stabit autem, potens est autem dominus rursum statuere illum (Rom. XIV). Considera quid dixerit: Potens est autem Dominus statuere illum. Non ille potens est, qui verba Domini praeterit.

XXV. Unde, fratres, magnopere devitemus alicujus mentem subvertere contra doctorem et monitorem suum; et meminerimus Scripturae dicentis: Libera cor tuum a malitia, ut salveris (Jer. IV). Nec pro obedientia superbiam et contumaciam in cordibus nostris invicem seminemus. Qui enim timet Dominum suum, si viderit fratrem suum errare et labi, magis debet monstrare quae sancta sunt, et rectum iter ostendere, ut cum omni castitate et tremore Dei incedens, illam Salomonis exsequatur sententiam: Libera eos qui ducuntur ad mortem, et redimere de interfectione non cesses (Prov. XXIII) Nec dicas, Nescio hunc. Scito quoniam Deus corda omnium novit. Et Judas in Epistola loquitur sua: Et hos quidem de igne rapientes, et odio habentes commaculatam tunicam (Jud. I). Caveamus hujuscemodi vestimentum, et induamur potius armaturam Dei, ut possimus resistere contra insidias diaboli. Non est enim nobis pugna contra carnem et sanguinem, sed adversus potestates et principatus, adversus rectores tenebrarum harum, adversus spiritalia nequitiae in coelestibus (Ephes. VI).

XXVI. Hoc quoque maxime providendum est, ne quis in alteram domum et in alterius cellulam commendet aliquid, et contra monasterii faciat disciplinam. Qui talis est, non est in numero fratrum, sed mercenarius et advena; nec Pascha Domini inter sanctos debet comedere, quia factus est lapis scandali in monasterio, et de eo posset dici: Lapides de via mea projicite (Jer. XX). Si enim levitonaria nostra, quando lavamus, sicca non fuerint, usque ad vesperam non habemus potestatem apud nos tenere, damusque Praeposito cui crediti sumus, vel ei cui creditum est cellarium, ut deferat ad eum locum, ubi vestimenta pariter omnium reservantur, et mane nobis dantur, ut expandamus illa ad solem, et cum sicca fuerint, non apud nos tenemus, sed damus in commune servanda, juxta praecepta majorum; quanto magis ea quae proprie visus es possidere, si alteri commendaveris, aut in tua volueris esse potestate, peccas in monasterii disciplinam, et non intelligis Paulum tibi loquentem: Vos autem in libertatem vocati estis, tantum ne libertate in occasionem carnis abutamini, sed charitate servite invicem (Gal. V). Et iterum: Dominus juxta est, nolite esse solliciti, sed estote in oratione intenti et deprecationibus (Phil. IV). Sciat quoque ille qui ab alio susceperit commendatum, et rem se arbitratur facere piam, ut fratrem refrigeret, quod peccet contra animam suam, subvertens regulam monasterii. O stulte, anima tua commissa est Praeposito tuo, et qui animam tuam corpusque custodit, indignus habebitur ut peritura conservet? Amemus justitiam, ut justificemur. Legimus enim: Misericordia occurrit his qui faciunt veritatem.

XXVII. Hoc quoque observandum est, ne quis stulta cogitatione deceptus, imo diaboli laqueis irretitus, dicat in corde suo: Quando moriar, tunc dono fratribus quod habuero. O stultissime hominum, ubi hoc scriptum invenisti? Nonne omnes sancti servientes Deo statim omnem saeculi sarcinam deposuerunt? Nonne in Actibus apostolorum, omnia quae habebant ad pedes apostolorum deferebant (Act. IV)? Aut quomodo poteris mortuus justitiae induere vestimentum, qui illud vivus habere non meruisti? Quare oblitus es illud, quod scriptum est: Quod seminaverit homo, hoc et metet (Gal. VI); et, Unusquisque recipiet, juxta quod egit (Ephes. VI); et, Reddet unicuique juxta opera sua (Rom. II); et iterum: Ego Dominus scrutans corda et probans renes, ut reddam unicuique juxta vias suas, et juxta fructum adinventionum ejus (Psal. LXI)? Quare nondum versaris in vita, et in hoc corpusculo constitutus non audis David loquentem: Thesaurizat, et ignorat cui congregat ea (Psal. CXLV), et sermonem evangelicum, avarum corripientem: Stulte, hac nocte animam expetent a te: quae autem praeparasti, cujus erunt (Luc. XII)? Et iterum: In illa die peribunt omnes cogitationes eorum. Stulte, quare non vis audire Dominum cohortantem: Vade, et vende omnia quae habes et da pauperibus, et tolle crucem tuam, et veni, et sequere me (Matth. XIX)? Quod adolescens audiens conversus est retro; non enim erat rectum cor ipsius, et ideo non potuit gravem divitiarum sarcinam deponere. Habebat quidem voluntatem, et Scriptura testatur, perfectae vitae, et splendore virtutum trahebatur ad laudem; sed retrahebant eum currentem divitiae, nec poterat Salvatoris audire doctrinam, quia adhuc de mundi deliciis cogitabat. Unde et Salvator loquitur: Difficile est eos, qui habent divitias, intrare in regna coelorum (Matth. XIX). Et iterum: Nemo potest duobus dominis servire: aut enim unum odio habebit, et alterum diliget; aut uni est obediens, et contemnet alterum. Non potestis Deo servire et mammonae (Luc. VI). Pharisaei autem cum essent avari, haec audiebant et irridebant: quorum incredulitatem devitemus, nec irridemus eos qui nos provocant. Renuntiemus mundo, ut perfecti perfectum sequamur thesaurum. Quorum animam possidet avaritia, his videtur pro Christo stulta paupertas. Quaestus est magnus pietas cum sufficientia. Nihil enim intulimus in hunc mundum, nec auferre quid possumus: habentes enim victum et vestitum, his contenti simus. Qui autem volunt divites fieri, incidunt in tentationem et laqueum, in concupiscentias multas, quae sunt stultae et noxiae, et demergunt homines in interitum et perditionem. Radix enim omnium malorum cupiditas (I Tim. VI).

XXVIII. Usque hodie Elias Israelem corripit dicens: Quousque claudicatis pede? Deus est, ite et sequimini eum (III Reg. XVIII). Et nobis loquitur: Si mandata sunt Dei, quae per Patrem nostrum tradidit nobis, et quae sequentes possumus pervenire ad regna coelorum, toto eadem desiderio compleamus: si autem sequimur cogitationes nostras, et ad aliud tendit animus, cur non errorem simpliciter confitemur, et ostendimus nos esse quod videri erubescimus? Ne forte dicatur et nobis: Quare polluistis locum meum sanctum (Ezech. XXII)? Et, Ejiciam eos e domo mea (Oseae, IX). Siquidem conciliabula monachorum vere Dei domus est, et sanctorum vinea, sicut scriptum legimus: Vinea facta est Salomoni in loco, qui vocatur Beelamon, dedit eam custodibus, unusquisque affert pro fructibus ejus mille argenteos. Vinea mea in conspectu meo est, mille Salomoni, et ducenti his qui custodiunt fructum ejus (Cant. VIII). Nec igitur polluentes eam projiciamur, sicut in Evangelio legimus ejectos esse de templo, qui vendebant in eo oves et boves; nummularios quoque ingrediens Dominus atque Salvator, et faciens sibi flagellum de funiculis, ejecit e templo, et fundens aera mensasque vendentium, et his qui vendebant columbas ait: Auferte haec omnia, et nolite facere domum Patris mei domum negotiationis. Scriptum est enim: Domus mea domus orationis vocabitur cunctis gentibus; vos autem fecistis eam speluncam latronum (Luc. XIX; Marc. XI). Et alibi: Propter vos nomen meum blasphematur in gentibus (Psal. LVI; Jer. VII).

XXIX. Obsecro vos, fratres, ne de nobis quoque dicatur: Alius quidem esurit, alius autem ebrius est: an domos non habet, ut bibatis et comedatis? Nisi forte Ecclesiam Dei contemnitis, et confunditis eos qui non habent; ad quos dicitur: Si quis esurit, domi comedat, ut non in judicium conveniatis (I Cor. XI). Non sit domus nostra vocis alienae, ne illud nobis congruenter aptetur: Opera Aegypti non abstulerunt a se. Et iterum: In praeceptis meis non ambulaverunt, et sabbata mea contaminaverunt; propterea cum clamaverint ad me, ego non exaudiam eos (Ezech. XX). Non permaneamus in cordis duritia, et ad iracundiam provocemus Deum, et fiat inimicus noster, et dicat: Ego autem dabo eis praecepta non bona, et justificationes in quibus non vivant (Ibid.); quia comederunt fructum mendacii, et adoraverunt opera manuum suarum, et repleta est terra eorum a principio augurio, ut terra alienigenarum.

TEACHING & DISCUSSION

XXX. Ne postquam renuntiaverimus saeculo, et coeperimus vexillum crucis sequi, iterum ad posteriora conversi, quaeramus refrigerium temporale, imitantes Ephraim dicentem: Dives factus sum, et inveni refrigerium mihi (Oseae XII); ne audiamus illud, quod et ille meruit audire: Omnes labores illius non inveniuntur prae iniquitatibus, in quibus peccavit. Et ne illud impleatur in nobis: Coepistis spiritu, et nunc carne consummamini: tanta passi estis sine causa (Gal. III)? Et ille contra nos sermo dicatur: Lex periit a sacerdote, et consilium a senioribus; et manus populi dissolutae sunt, senes de porta quieverunt, electi a psalmis suis cessaverunt (Ezech. VII). Rursumque dicatur: Propter vos nomen meum blasphematur in gentibus (Rom. II): et contemptis institutionibus Patris nostri subrepat oblivio, mediatoremque Dei atque sanctorum nostro vitio negligamus.

XXXI. Quis enim fructus, aut quod signum praeceptorum Dei inveniatur in nobis, aut in quo professionem impleamus arreptam? Nonne omnia dimisimus, et avaritiae subjacemus, et dicitur nobis: Unde bella, et pugnae (Jac. IV)? Nonne ex avaritia? Nam quia unusquisque quaerit utilitatem suam, non proximi, usque hodie vivens Ezechiel prophetali sermone nos corripit dicens: Negationes erant in te. Filius inhonorat patrem, et Pater exprobrat filio (Ezech. XXVII). Quid in die judicii respondebimus, aut quid in novissimo tempore pro defensione nostra poterimus obtendere? Haec omnia facta sunt nobis, quia Sacerdotes plauserunt manibus, et populus dilexit similiter. Quia sicut populus, sic sacerdos (Jer. V). Propterea reddam ei, inquit, secundum vias suas, et cogitationes illius restituam ei (Oseae IV).

XXXII. Non de omnibus vobis haec loquor, sed de his qui majorum praecepta contemnunt; multoque melius erat illis ignorare viam justitiae, quam scientes reverti ab eo quod traditum est illis sancto mandato (II Petr. II). De hujuscemodi hominibus moerens Jeremias scribit: Defecerunt in lacrymis oculi mei, conturbatus est venter meus, effusa est in terra gloria mea, super contritione filiae populi mei; quia defecit parvulus et lactens in plateis civitatis. Matribus suis dixerunt: Ubi est triticum et vinum? cum deficerent quasi vulnerati in plateis urbis, cum funderent animas suas in sinu matrum suarum (Thren. II). Scimus quod non in fortitudine equi velit Deus, neque in femoribus viri sibi complaceat (Psal. CXLVI).

TEACHING & DISCUSSION

XXXIII. Et idcirco revertamur ad Dominum Deum nostrum, ut quando oraverimus, exaudiat nos qui quotidie hortatur ut vacemus et cognoscamus eum. Et alibi loquitur: Revertimini ad me, et ego revertar ad vos. Et iterum: Revertimini ad me, filii recedentes, et ego dominabor vestri (Jer. III). Ezechiel similiter contestatur ac dicit: Quare moriemini, domus Israel? Nolo mortem peccatoris, sed tantum ut revertatur de via mala sua, et vivat (Ezech. XVIII). Et clementissimus ac totius honitatis caput clamat in Evangelio ad nos Dominus atque testatur: Venite ad me, omnes qui laboratis et onerati estis, et ego reficiam vos. Tollite jugum meum super vos, et discite a me, quia mitis sum et humilis corde, et invenietis requiem animabus vestris (Matth. XI). Consideremus quod bonitas Dei ad poenitentiam nos provocet, et sancti viri cohortantur ad salutem. Non induremus corda nostra, neque thesaurizemus iram nobis in die irae et revelationis justi judicii Dei, qui reddet unicuique juxta opera sua (Rom. II); sed ex toto corde revertamur ad Dominum, et secundum Moysi verba memorantis: Si revertaris ad Dominum ex toto corde tuo, mundabit cor tuum, et cor seminis tui (Deut. XXX).

XXXIV. Laboremus sicut boni milites Christi, et observemus illud quod scriptum est: Nemo militans Deo implicat se negotiis saecularibus, ut ei cui militat placeat (II Tim. II). Si autem quis et in agone contendat, non coronatur nisi legitime certaverit. Laborantem agricolam oportet primum de fructibus ejus participare. Scriptum est: Omnes populi ibunt unusquisque in viam suam. Nos autem in nomine Domini Dei nostri magnificabimur; ipsi impediti sunt et ceciderunt, nos autem surreximus et erecti sumus (Psal. XIX).

XXXV. Qui ambulat in die, non impingit; qui autem in nocte graditur, impingit, quia lumen non est in eo (Joan. XI). Nos autem, sicut dixit Apostolus, non sumus filii praevaricationis in perditionem, sed fidei in acquisitionem animae (Heb. X). Et alibi: Omnes, inquit, filii lucis estis, et filii Dei (I Thes. III). Non sumus filii noctis, neque tenebrarum. Si ergo sumus filii lucis, debemus scire quae lucis sunt, et facere fructus luminis in omni opere bono: quod enim manifestatur, lux est. Si in toto corde revertamur ad Dominum, et in praeceptis sanctorum illius et Patris nostri simplici corde conversamur, abundabimus in omni opere bono. Quod si superemur carnis voluptatibus, in die quasi in media nocte parietem palpabimus: et non inveniemus viam civitatis et habitaculi nostri, de quo dicitur: Esurientium et sitientium anima deficit (Psalm. CVI); quia contempserunt legem sibi a Deo traditam, et vocem prophetarum non audierunt: et idcirco non potuerunt ad promissam requiem pervenire.

XXXVI. Vigilemus et attenti simus: si enim naturalibus non pepercit, nec nobis parcet. Non de cunctis, sed de negligentibus loquor, quibus jure aptabitur illa deploratio: Vae eis qui recesserunt a me. Manifesti sunt, quia impie egerunt in me, quia dereliquerunt me fontem aquae vivae, et foderunt sibi contritos lacus, qui non possunt aquam continere (Jer. II). Et quia non audierunt judices ejus, audiant dicentem Deum: Constitui super vos speculatores. Audite vocem tubae. Et dixerunt: Non audiemus (Jer. II). Unde ista incredulitas? Nonne ex eo quia alienos cognoverunt, et non adversati sunt? Loquitur et alibi Spiritus sanctus per prophetam: Ego enim sum Deus Dominus tuus, qui formavi coelum, et creavi terram; cujus manus condiderunt omnem coeli militiam, et non ostendit ea tibi, ut ambulares post illam (Isai. XLV). Quod quidem et per Moysem praecepit, dicens: Non cum suspexeris coelum, et videris solem et lunam ac stellas, et omne ornamentum coeli, errore coeli deceptus adores ea (Deut. IV). Ego sum Deus, qui eduxi te de terra Aegypti, et Deum extra me nescis, et qui salvos posset facere, non est praeter me. Ego sum, qui te pavi in solitudine, in terra inhabili, et impleti sunt saturitate, et elevata sunt corda eorum (Exod. XX). Idcirco obliti sunt mei, et ego tradam eos dispersioni in gentibus cunctis (Jer. IX).

XXXVII. Quae audientes quasi de somno expergiscamur, et praebeamus nos dignos Domini servituti, ut misereatur et dicat nobis: Invocate me, et ego exaudiam vos. Ipse enim ait: Qui dispersit Israel, congregavit eum. Et alibi: Non faciam, inquit, juxta iram furoris mei, nec sic relinquam, ut deleam Ephraim. Et iterum: Non in aeternum puniam vos, nec semper irascar vobis. Spiritus enim a me egreditur, et omne quod spirat ego feci. Et in eodem loco jungit ac dicit: Dedi eis consolationem veram, pacem super pacem his qui erant prope et longe: dixitque Dominus: Sanabo eos (Jer. XXXI). Cujus ut plene misericordiam cognoscamus, Jeremiae sermone docet, dicens: Si elevatum fuerit coelum in sublime, et si humiliatum pavimentum terrae deorsum, ego non replebo gentem Israel pro omnibus quae fecerunt (Jer. III).

XXXVIII. Cumque tanta clementia sit Salvatoris Domini, et nos provocet ad salutem, convertamus corda nostra ad eum: Quia jam hora est, ut de somno evigilemus; nox praecessit, dies autem appropinquavit; deponamus ergo opera tenebrarum, et in duamur arma lucis (Rom. XIII). Filioli mei, primum ex toto corde diligamus Deum, deinde nosmetipsos amemus mutuo, memores praeceptorum Dei Salvatoris, in quibus ait: Pacem meam do vobis, pacem meam relinquo vobis: non sicut mundus dat pacem, ego do vobis. In his enim duobus mandatis tota lex pendet, et prophetae (Joan. XIV).

XXXIX. Si quis in domo monasterii sub Praeposito manens, nulla re indigens quam in monasterio habere permissum est, et habet patrem fratremque et amicum charissimum, nihil ab eis penitus accipiat, non tunicam, non palliolum, non aliam quamlibet rem. Si autem comprobatum fuerit quod minus habeat de his quae praecepta sunt, culpa omnis atque correctio ad Praepositum convertetur.

XL. Vos igitur qui estis principes monasteriorum, si quos aliqua re videritis indigere, et esse in angustia constitutos, nolite eos negligere, scientes vos reddituros rationem pro omni grege, super quem vos Spiritus sanctus constituit inspicere, et pascere Ecclesiam Dei, quam acquisivit proprio sanguine (Act. XX). Propterea nos, qui fortiores sumus, debemus infirmitates invalidorum portare, et non nobismetipsis placere, sed proximo in bono ad aedificationem. Nam et Christus non sibi placuit, sed sicut scriptum est. Opprobria exprobrantium tibi ceciderunt super me (Rom. XV). Et iterum: Non quaero, inquit, quod mihi expedit, sed quod omnibus, ut salvi fiant (I Cor. XX)

XLI. Si autem Dominus ac Salvator noster ita praecipit, et sancti ita conversati sunt, patres quoque nostri ita nos docuerunt, consurgamus a somno, et quae sunt nobis praecepta faciamus. Quaecunque scripta sunt, ad nostram eruditionem scripta sunt, ut per patientiam et consolationem Scripturarum spem habeamus (Rom. XV), et nullus nostrum causa sit erroris alieni, nec aemulemur eos qui prospere agunt in vita sua. Cum enim omnia necessaria carni fuerint consecuti, morientes nihil secum asportabunt. Filii saeculi hujus habent in hoc saeculo fiduciam, quoniam de mundo sunt, et mundus amat quod suum est. Qui autem filii Dei sunt, illius sermonis evangelici recordantur:

Si mundus vos odit, scitote quod me primum oderit (Joan. XV). Et iterum: Qui voluerit esse amicus hujus mundi, inimicus fiet Deo. Et rursum: Tribulationem habebitis: sed confidite, ego vici mundum. Et iterum: Beati qui lugent, quoniam ipsi consolabuntur. Beati qui esuriunt et sitiunt justitiam, quoniam ipsi saturabuntur. Beati qui persecutionem patiuntur propter justitiam, quoniam ipsorum est regnum coelorum (Matth. V). De filiis autem noctis quid e contrario dicitur? Nonne illud? Vae vobis, divites, quoniam recepistis consolationem vestram. Vae vobis qui saturati estis nunc, quia esurietis. Vae vobis qui nunc ridetis, quia lugebitis ac flebitis (Luc. VI).

XLII. Quamobrem mundi amicitias devitemus, ut illud mereamur audire: Ad vesperam demorabitur fletus, et ad matutinum laetitia. Audivit Dominus, et misertus est mei. Scidisti saccum meum, et accinxisti me laetitia. Quis enim sanctorum non in luctu ac tristitia per mundi hujus transivit viam? Jeremias: Non sedi, inquit, cum consilio ludentium, sed tremebam a facie manus tuae. Solus sedebam, quoniam amaritudine repletus sum (Jer. XV). David quoque scribit: Quasi lugens ac moerens sic humiliabar (Psal. XXXIV). Quorum nos vestigiis insistentes intelligimus quod salus nostra in tempore tribulationis sit, et prophetae pollicitatio impleatur dicentis: Non relinquuntur, qui in angustia sunt usque ad tempus. Si ergo habet tempus tribulatio et angustia, et non erit sempiterna, seminemus in lacrymis, et metamus in gaudio, non deficientes; quod noverimus Dominum de tentatione liberare cultores suos.

XLIII. Dominus pater noster est; Dominus judex noster est; Dominus princeps, Dominus rex noster; Dominus ipse nos salvabit; cujus praecepta si neglexerimus, permanebimus in angustia. Ipse enim dicit: Qui sequuntur me, possidebunt terram, et haereditabunt montem sanctum meum (Isai. LVII): quem et nos possidebimus, si impleamus legem ejus, et audiamus illud quod dicitur: Mundas facite in conspectu ejus vias vestras. Et iterum: Tollite offendicula de via populi mei. Et alibi: Ejicite de consilio pestilentem, et egredietur cum eo contentio (Jer. XV). Qui justum dicit injustum, et injustum judicat justum, uterque in conspectu Dei immundus est. Caveamus ne dicatur et de nobis: Filii alienati sunt ei (Psal. XVII). Et illud: Filiae Sion elevatae sunt, et ambulaverunt in excelso collo, et in superbia oculorum, trahentes pedibus tunicas, et pedibus simul ludentes (Isai. III), et in correptione nostra rursum prophetalis sermo concordet, dicens: Quomodo facta est meretrix civitas fidelis

Sion, plena judicio, in qua justitia dormit? Nunc autem latrones (Isai. I). Et: Populus intelligens commiscebatur meretrici. Tu ergo, Israel, ne ignoraberis (Oseae IV). Si vero divina meditemur, poterimus illud dicere, quod et David: Exsultabo super eloquia tua, sicut qui invenit spolia multa (Psal. CXVIII). Et: Quam dulcia gutturi meo eloquia tua, super mel et favum ori meo. Cantabiles mihi erant justificationes tuae in loco peregrinationis meae (Psal. CX). Et in alio loco: Non proposui ante oculos meos rem iniquam: facientes iniquitatem odio habui. Et non adhaesit mihi cor pravum, declinantes a me malignos non agnoscebam; detrahentem in absconso proximo suo, hunc persequebar, superbo oculo et insatiabili corde cum hoc simul non edebam. Oculi mei super fideles terrae, ut facerem eos sedere mecum.

XLIV. Quorum omnium nos imitemur opera, ut sit in diebus nostris pax et justitia, et non nobis illud eveniat, quod alibi legimus: Super terra populi mei spinae et fenum consurgent (Isai. XXXII). Sed magis innovemus nobis novalia, et non seminemus super spinas. Cumque custodierimus quae mandata sunt nobis, manifesti erimus quod diligamus Deum, sicut testatur et in alio loco Scriptura divina: Qui audit mandata mea et servat ea, ille est qui diligit me. Qui autem diliget me, diligetur a Patre meo, et ego diligam eum, et veniemus ego et Pater meus, et mansionem apud eum faciemus, et ostendam ei meipsum (Joan. XIV). Et, Vos amici mei estis, si feceritis quae praecipio vobis (Joan. XV). Tollamus nobiscum multos sermones, et convertamur ad Dominum Deum nostrum, et dicamus ei: Potes dimittere peccata, ut accipiamus bona, et reddamus ei fructum labiorum nostrorum (Oseae XIV), et delectetur in nobis anima nostra.

XLV. Atque utinam poeniteat nos erroris et negligentiae, et conversi ad priora dicamus: Assur non salvabit nos; super equos non ascendemus; nec jam dicemus: Dii nostri opera manuum nostrarum. Deus qui in te est miserebitur pupilli, sanabo habitacula eorum (Oseae XIV). Rursumque dicet de nobis: Diligam eos manifeste, et avertam iram meam ab eis. Ero quasi ros; Israel florebit ut lilium, et mittet radices suas quasi Libanus. Ibunt rami ejus, et erit quasi oliva fructifera, et odor ejus ut thuris. Revertentur et sedebunt unusquisque in tabernaculis suis, et vivent, et confirmabuntur frumento: florebit sicut vinea memoria eorum, sicut odor thuris Ephraim. Quid ei et idolis? Ego humiliabo eum, et confortabo eum. Ego ut juniperus condensa; ex me fructus ejus inventus est. Quis sapiens, et intelligit haec; aut intelligens, et cognoscit ista (Ibid.)? Atque utinam et nos ex eo fructum afferre valeamus, sine quo nihil boni operis fieri potest.

XLVI. Revertamur ad Dominum, ut de nobis quoque possit dicere: Peccatorum et iniquitatis eorum memor amplius non ero (Isai. XLIII). Non relinquamus legem Dei, quam Pater noster ab eo accipiens nobis tradidit, neque parvi ejus mandata pendamus; ne et super nos planctus ille dicatur: Quomodo obscuratum est aurum, et immutatum argentum bonum: effusi sunt lapides sancti in omni viarum principio (Thren. IV)? Nec post plurimos labores Patris nostri, quos pro salute nostra suscepit, seipsum exemplum virtutis tribuens, glorians de nobis, et apud sanctos loquens. Isti filii mei sunt, et populus meus filii mei, et non denegabunt; et post hujuscemodi testimonium non perdamus fiduciam bonae conscientiae, spoliati vestibus quibus nos induit; et introducti ab eo in stadium, ut legitime certemus, non superemur ab inimicis nostris. Et postquam venerimus ad illud tempus quo egrediamur de corpore, ne inimici efficiamur Patris nostri thesauris servientes: ut qui jejuniis et afflictione corporis debuimus acquirere animae libertatem, carni et deliciis, et pulchrioribus vestimentis, stratisque mollioribus nos dedicemus, non solum ipsi pereuntes, sed et alios qui proficere potuerunt exemplo nostro ducentes ad ruinam, de quibus scriptum est: Non accepistis spiritum servitutis timorem (Rom. VIII), sed fortitudinis, et charitatis, et pudicitiae. Et: Cibus nos non commendat Deo. Neque enim si comederimus, abundabimus: nec si non comederimus, indigebimus. Non est enim regnum Dei cibus et potus, sed justitia, gaudium, et pax in Spiritu sancto (Rom. XIV). Qui in hoc servit Christo, placet Deo, probatus est omnibus. Isaias quoque dicit: Qui exspectant Lominum, immutabunt virtutem, assument pennas ut aquilae; current, et laborabunt; gradientur, et non esurient (Isai. XL). Idcirco elevabit signum in gentes, et congregabit profugos Israel. Cito velociter venient: non esurient, neque dormitabunt. Non dormient, nec solvent zonas de lumbis suis, neque rumpentur in calceamentis eorum corrigiae. Quorum jacula acuta sunt, et intenti arcus; pedes equorum, ut petra fortissima: rotae curruum quasi tempestas; impetum facient ut leones, et aderant ut catuli leonum (Ibid. V).

XLVII. Et nos igitur sanctorum imitatores simus, nec obliviscamur institutionis, qua nos erudivit Pater noster, dum adhuc esset in corpore. Ne exstinguamus lucernam ardentem, quam posuit super capita nostra. Ad cujus lumen hujus saeculi incedentes, meminerimus, quod per studium illius Deus nos in propriam familiam receperit, peregrenis hospitium tribuens, in maris turbinibus constitutis portum ostendens, panem in fame, umbram in aestu, vestimentum in nuditate; imperitos praeceptis spiritalibus erudivit; vitiis servientes castitate circumdedit; procul positos sibi junxit. Ne post illius dormitionem obliviscamur tantae bonitatis et beneficiorum immortalium, vertentes furorem in judicium, et fructum justitiae in amaritudinem, et loquatur contra nos: Judicate inter me et vineam meam. Exspectavi ut faceret fructum, et fecit iniquitatem, et non justitiam, sed clamorem (Isai. V); et veniat super nos illa maledictio, quam prophetalis sermo ille prosequitur, et quam omni studio fugere ac vitare debemus, sequentes conversationem eorum qui nos in Domino praecesserunt Patrum pariter ac fratrum: qui renuntiantes saeculo, et inoffenso ad Dominum pergentes gradu, nunc ejus haereditate potiuntur: quam vereor ne perdamus nostra desidia, et illud nobis propheticum aptetur, quod dictum est in Ephraim: Oleum in Aegyptum mercatur (Oseae XXII). Mixti sunt in gentibus, et didicerunt opera eorum (Psal. CV). Ne postquam vocati sumus in libertatem, sicut scriptum est: Tollam vos unum de populo, et duos de familia, et inducam vos in Sion, et dabo vobis pastores secundum cor meum, qui pascant vos cum disciplina (Jer. III); resolvantur vincula charitatis, et dicatur de nobis: Filius glorificat patrem, et servus dominum suum. Si pater ego sum, ubi est gloria mea? Si Dominus, ubi est timor meus (Malach. I)?

XLVIII. Idcirco unusquisque nostrum clamat ad Dominum: Muri Sion deducant sicut torrentes iacrymas die ac nocte. Ne des requiem tibi, neque taceat pupilla oculi tui. Surge, et lauda in nocte, in principio vigiliarum tuarum: effunde sicut aquam cor tuum in conspectu Domini. Leva ad illum manus tuas pro animabus parvulorum tuorum, qui defecerunt in capite universorum gressuum (Thren. II). Ne illud contra nos dicatur: Luxit et corruptus est orbis. Luxerunt excelsi terrae, et terra impie egit propter habitatores suos: dereliquerunt enim legem, et immutaverunt praecepta mea testamentum aeternum. Idcirco maledictio devorabit terram, quia peccaverunt habitatores ejus, et dereliquerunt homines pauci (Isai. XXIV). Ne et nostrum vinum lugeat et vinea, et ingemiscant, qui prius toto animo laetabantur, dicaturque de nobis: In domo insaniam confinxerunt, corrupti sunt sicut dies collis. Aut illud:

Captio ex vobis est. Et, Dixistis enim, fecimus testamentum cum inferno, et cum morte pactum (Isai. XXVIII). Quae verba vitantes, credimus magis, quod in tempore suo Orietur stella ex Jacob, et exsurget homo de Israel, qui percutiet principes Moab, et filios Seth (Num. XXIV). Ut non sit in domo Israel stimulus furoris, et spina doloris (Ezech. XXVIII). Quia facta est Domino pars ejus Jacob, funiculus haereditatis ejus Israel (Deut. XXXII). Et alibi loquitur Jeremias: Si cessaverit in conspectu meo lex ista, gens etiam Israel cessare poterit (Jer. XXXI). Et rursum: Dabo laborem eorum justis, et tastamentum aeternum ponam cum ipsis, et scietur in gentibus semen eorum, ac nepotes. Omnis, qui viderit eos, cognoscet, quia isti sunt semen a Domino benedictum, et gaudia perfruentur Domini (Isai. LXI).

XLIX. Et nos ergo scrutemur vias nostras, et gressus dijudicemus, et sequamur odorem scientiae: abscondentes semper verba ejus in cordibus nostris, ut simus immaculati in via, et in lege Domini ambulemus. Non nos terreat fragilitas corporis, et longi temporis labor. Patres vestri ubi sunt, et Prophetae, ut scriptum est, nunquid aeternum vivent? Verba autem mea et legitima mea suscipite, quae ego praecipio in Spiritu meo servis meis prophetis, qui fuerunt cum patribus vestris (Zach. I). Sentiamus ineffabilem clementiam Dei nostri, qui usque hodie ad poenitentiam nos hortatur, dicens: Nunquid qui cadet non resurget? aut qui aversatur, non revertetur? Quare aversatus est populus meus aversione impudenti, et obtinuerunt in voluptatibus suis, et noluerunt reverti (Jer. VIII)? Si reversi fuerimus ad eum, aedificabit nos Spiritu suo, juxta illud quod scriptum est: Aedificans Hierusalem Dominus, dispersiones Israelis congregabit (Psal. CXLVI).

L. Quod autem nostri coetus et communio ex Deo sit, qua nos invicem copulamur, Apostolus nos docuit dicens: Bonorum operum communionis oblivisci nolite, talibus enim victimis placatur Deus (Hebr. XIII). In Actibus apostolorum quoque idem legimus: Multitudinis autem credentium erat cor unum et anima una, et nullus suum quid dicebat, sed erant eis universa communia. Et virtute magna dabant apostoli testimonium resurrectionis Domini Jesu (Act. IV). Et Psalmista in eadem verba consensit, dicens: Ecce quam bonum, et quam jucundum, habitare fratres in unum (Psal. CXXXII). Et nos in coenobiis commorantes, et nobis mutua charitate sociati, demus studium, ut quomodo sanctorum Patrum in hac vita meruimus consortium, ita in futuro quoque participes eorum simus: scientes quod crux vitae nostrae doctrinaeque principium sit, et oporteat nos cum Christo pati, et nosse, quod absque tribulationibus et angustiis nullus victoriam consequatur. Beatus vir qui suffert tentationem, quia cum probatus fuerit, coronam vitae accipiet (Jac. IV). Et iterum: Laboravit in saeculum, et vivet in aeternum. Si tamen compatimur, ut et glorificemur. Aestimo, inquit, quod non sunt condignae passiones hujus temporis ad futuram gloriam, quae revelabitur in nobis (Rom. VIII). Et alibi scriptum est: Existimavi, ut cognoscerem hoc, labor est in conspectu meo (Psal. LXXII). Et iterum: Ego laboravi sequens te, et diem hominum non consideravi (Jer. XVII). Et alio loco: Multae tribulationes justorum, et ex omnibus his liberabit eos Dominus (Psal. XXXIII). Et Dominus noster loquitur in Evangelio: Qui perseveraverit usque in finem, hic salvus erit (Matth. X). Et alibi: Hic est liber mandatorum, et lex scripta in sempiternum. Omnes qui observaverint eam, vivent; qui autem dereliquerint, morientur. Revertere, Jacob, et apprehende eum; ambula in splendore luminis ejus, et non des alteri gloriam tuam, et ea quae conducunt tibi, genti alienae. Beati sumus, Israel, quia placita Deo nostro nota sunt nobis. Confide, popule meus, memoriabilis Israel (Baruch. IV). Et iterum Isaias loquitur: Laetare, Israel, et festum agite diem, omnes qui diligitis eum. Gaudete, qui confiditis in eo, ut fugatis, et impleamini ex uberibus consolationis ejus (Isai. LXVI).

LI. Habeamus curam legendarum et discendarum Scripturarum, et in earum semper meditatione versemur, scientes scriptum: Ex fructu oris sui vir saturabitur, et merces labiorum ejus reddetur (Prov. XIII). Haec sunt quae nos ducunt ad aeternam vitam quae nobis tradidit Pater noster et jugiter meditanda praecepit; ut impleatur illud in nobis, quod scriptum est: Erunt haec verba, quae ego praecipio tibi hodie, in corde tuo et in anima tua; docebis ea filios tuos, et loqueris in eis sedens in domo, et ambulans in via, et accubans, atque consurgens. Scribe ea pro signo in manu tua, et erunt immobilia ante oculos tuos. Scribes quoque ea in postibus domuum tuarum, et in liminibus, ut discatis timere Dominum cunctis diebus quibus vivitis (Deut. XI). Salomon quoque ipsum significans dicit: Scribe ea in latitudine cordis tui (Prov. III).

LII. Considerate quantis testimoniis ad meditationem sacrarum Scripturarum nos sermo Domini cohortetur, ut quae ore volvimus, corde possideamus. Bonum est homini, cum levaverit jugum ab adolescentia sua. Sedebit solitarius et tacebit, quoniam levabit super se jugum, dabit percutienti se maxillam, saturabitur opprobriis, quoniam non semper abjiciet Dominus (Thren. III). Et alibi scriptum est: Recordatus sum misericordiae infantiae tuae. Et iterum: Laetare, juvenis, in adolescentia tua, et exsultet cor tuum in diebus juventutis tuae, et ambula in viis cordis tui absque macula, et in conspectu oculorum tuorum, et scito quoniam in omnibus his adducat te Dominus in judicio. Aufer furorem a corde tuo, et malitiam a carne tua, quoniam adolescentia et stultitia vanitas est (Eccl. XI). Et, Memento creatoris tui in diebus adolescentiae tuae, donec veniant dies pessimi, et occupent anni, in quibus dices: Non est mihi in eis voluntas; donec obtenebrescat sol, et lux, et luna, et stellae, et convertantur nubes post pluviam. In die qua movebuntur custodes domus, et subvertentur viri virtutis, et cessent molentes, quia paucae factae sunt; et obscurabuntur, quae vident in foraminibus, et claudent vias in foro in infirmitate vocis molentis. Et exsurgent ad vocem passeris, et humiliabuntur omnes filii cantici. Et quidem ab alto aspicient, et pavores in via, et floreat amygdalum, et ingrassetur locusta, et scindatur capparis. Quoniam abiit homo in domum saeculi sui, et gyraverunt in foro qui plangunt, quoadusque evertatur funiculus argenti, et conteratur monile auri, et confringatur hydria ad fontem, et impediatur rota super lacum, et convertatur pulvis in terram, sicut fuit, et spiritus revertatur ad Dominum, qui dedit eum (Ibid. XII). In Evangelio quoque scriptum est: Pueri, nunquid habetis pulmentum? Mittite in dexteram partem navis, et invenietis (Joan. XXI). Et iterum: Omnis puer ac juvenculus, qui nescit hodie bonum ac malum, ipsi intrabunt in terram bonam. Ac rursum: Omne masculinum quod aperit vulvam, sanctum vocabitur (Exod. LIV). Et in Evangelio: Puer autem ibat, et crescebat, et proficiebat apud Deum et apud homines (Luc. II). Jesus quoque minister Moysi juvenis erat, et non egrediebatur de tabernaculo Dei. Et de David scriptum legimus: Puer flavi coloris, elegantibus oculis (I Reg. XVI). Timotheus quoque adhuc puer et adolescens sacris litteris eruditus est, ut ad fidem Domini Salvatoris illarum semita perveniret. Et de Daniele, quia eruditus erat, scriptum legimus, quod vir desideriorum appellatus sit (Dan. X). Joseph quoque erat dilectissimus patri suo, quoniam ejus imperiis serviebat, et decem ac septem adhuc natus annos praecepta illius legem vitae suae arbitrabatur.

LIII. Et haec cuncta replicavi, ut sanctorum vitas considerantes, non circumferamur omni vento doctrinae (Ephes. IV), sed laboremus, et eorum conversationem nostrae vitae propositum habeamus exemplum, ut simus populus Dei peculiaris. Nec contristemus Spiritum sanctum, in quo signati sumus in die redemptionis; ne illum exstinguamus in nobis: et prophetias non contemnamus; ne forsitan volenti Spiritui sancto habitare in nobis non demus locum. Nullum alium timeamus, praeter Deum, qui ultor et judex est operum singulorum, et cum sancto sanctus est, et cum viro innocente innocens (Psal. XVII); et dicit: Ego amantes me diligo, et qui me quaerent invenient gaudium (Prou. VIII). Et alibi loquitur: Si ambulaveritis contra me perversi, ego ambulabo contra vos perversus (Lev. XXVI).

LIV. Non irascamur invicem (Psal. IV): etiamsi ira nos vicerit, non peccemus irati, solis occubitum poenitentia praeoccupantes (Matth. XVIII). Meminerimus esse praeceptum, quoties peccanti in nos ignoscere debemus, et munus nostrum relinquere ante altare: quod nequaquam suscipitur, si non fuerit reconciliatione placabile (Ibid. V): ut possimus dicere: Dimitte nobis debita nostra, sicut et nos dimittimus debitoribus nostris (Luc. XI). Et Apostolus praecepit: Si quis habet adversus aliquem querimoniam, sicut et Christus donavit nobis, sic facite (Col. V). Simus discipuli mansuetudinis sanctorum omnium, et praecipue David, de quo scriptum est: Memento, Domine, David, et omnis mansuetudinis ejus (Psal. CXXXI). Et Moysi, de quo legitur, quod fuerit mansuetus super omnem terram (Num. XII). Et Dominus in Evangelio de mansuetis ac mitibus loquitur: Beati mansueti et mites corde, quoniam ipsi possidebunt terram (Matth. V). Magnae sapientiae est, mansuetudinem possidere, et audire: Sapiens esto, fili, ut laetetur cor meum (Prov. X). Et iterum: Imitatores estote Dei, filii charissimi (Ephes. V). Et, Estote perfecti, sicut et Pater vester, qui in coelis est, perfectus est (Marc. V). Et alibi: Sancti estote, quoniam ego sanctus sum, dicit Dominus (Lev. V).

LV. Quae legentes testimonia, seminemus nobis justitiam, ut metamus fructum vitae. Illuminemus lucem scientiae, quia tempus est ut cognoscamus Deum, donec veniat fructus justitiae nobis. Ecce nunc tempus acceptabile, et dies salutis (II Cor. VI). Et vere, secundum quod scriptum est, Plenitudo legis est dilectio (Rom. XIII). Joanne in haec eadem concinente: Hoc praeceptum accepimus a Patre, ut diligatis invicem (Joan. XV). Et, Qui diligit Deum, diligat et fratrem suum (II Joan. IV). Et, Non sicut Cain, qui ex maligno erat, occidit fratrem suum. Et quare occidit? quia opera ejus maligna erant; fratris autem ejus bona. Non admiremur, fratres, si oderit nos mundus: nos scimus, quia transivimus de morte ad vitam, eo quod diligamus fratres (I Joan. III). Ergo diligamus nos mutuo.

LVI. Loquar aliud ad vos audentius, filii charissimi. Ex quo credidit mihi Deus conversationis vestrae et sanctae conversationis gregem, non cessavi lacrymis monere, et docere singulos, ut placeatis Deo; nec subtraxi aliquid, quod vobis utile sentiebam, ut dicerem: Et nunc commendo vos Deo, et verbo gratiae ejus, qui potest vos aedificare, et dare vobis haereditatem cum sanctis (Act. XX). Vigilate, omni studio curaque contendite, ne obliviscamini propositi vestri, sed implete quod vos scitis esse pollicitos. Ego enim jam delibor, et tempus resolutionis meae adest: qui certamen bonum ex parte certavi, cursum consummavi, fidem servavi. De caetero reposita est mihi corona justitiae, quam reddet mihi Dominus in illa die justus judex: non solum mihi, sed et omnibus qui dilexerunt justitiam ejus (II Tim. IV), et omnia Patris mandata fecerunt. Finis verbi: omnia audi, Deum time, et mandata ejus custodi; quoniam omnis homo: universum opus Deus adducet in judicium, sive bonum, sive malum sit (Eccl. XII). Explicit doctrina sancti Orsiesii.

The Scriptorium Project is the work of a small group of lay people of various apostolic churches who are interested in the preservation, transmission, and translation of the works of the early and medieval church. Our efforts are to make the works of the church fathers accessible to anyone who might have an interest in Christian antiquities and the theological, philosophical, and moral writings that have become the bedrock of Western Civilization.

To-date, our releases have pulled from the Greek, Syriac, Georgian, Latin, Celtic, Ethiopian, and Coptic traditions of Christianity, and have been pulled from sundry local traditions and languages.

TEACHING & DISCUSSION

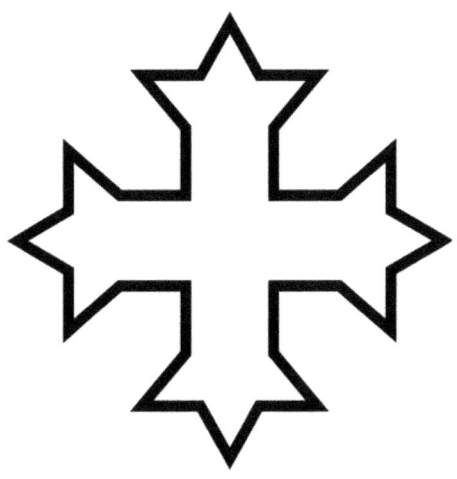

Nile River Valley Church Series (Coptic, Nubian, Ethiopian):

Teaching & Discussion by St. Orsisius of Tabenna (Feb. 2008)
The Holy Ghost by St. Didymas the Blind (Sept. 2008)
Rule of St. Macarius by St. Macarius of Egypt (Apr. 2009)
Letter to Leo by St. Proterius of Alexandria (June 2009)
The Paradise of Heraclides by Heraclides of Alexandria (Apr. 2013)
Discourse on Mary Theotokos by St. Cyril of Jerusalem (Sept. 2013)
Nicene Canons in the Old Nubian Language (Jan. 2018)
First Book of Ethiopian Maccabees (Dec 2018)
Life of St. Mary the Egyptian by St. Sophronius of Jerusalem (May 2019)
The Old Nubian Miracle of St. Mena (Jan. 2021)
Two Letters by St. Dionysius of Alexandria (Apr. 2022)
Instructions: Counsel for Novices by St. Ammonas the Hermit (Sept 2022)
Religious Exercise and Quiet by St. Isaiah the Solitary (Oct 2022)
The Vision of Theophilus by St. Cyril of Alexandria (Dec 2022)
Second Book of Ethiopian Maccabees (Aug 2023)

www.ingramcontent.com/pod-product-compliance
Lightning Source LLC
LaVergne TN
LVHW052004060526
838201LV00059B/3825